HEROES AND OTHER FOLKS

by

Jim Joseph

FIRST EDITION

UNIVERSITY EDITIONS, Inc.
59 Oak Lane, Spring Valley
Huntington, West Virginia 25704

Cover by Brendon and Brian Fraim

Columns in this book originally appeared in the *Daily Times*, Portsmouth, Ohio; *The Ironton Tribune*, Ironton, Ohio; and *The Messenger*, Troy, Ala.

Copyright 1997, by Jim Joseph
Library of Congress Catalog Card No: 96-90587
ISBN: 1-56002-698-7

Dedication

To my toughest editor, severest critic, biggest fan and wife of 45 years, Norma Helen Johnson Joseph—without whom nothing in my adult life would have been possible.

CONTENTS

1-Fun and games

Where have all the heroes gone?   6
Kathie Lee is a Super singer   7
Roy still reigns as King of the Cowboys   9
Namesake of a legend   10
9 holes a year, that's par for me   12
The big ones always get away   13
The Wonders of basketball   15
Forget luge, go for a snooze   17
Hunters, don't forget to take your lunch   18
XXVII reasons not to watch the game   20
One strike ends, time for another   21

2-D.C.(entralize it)

George and Abe deserve better   25
A write-in vote for a special stamp   26
Counting noses, asking questions   28
Spare the rod . . . you know the rest   29
Debates? Comic has a better idea   31
If this is a joke, no one is laughing   33
One of the Michaels on a big-bucks bill?   34
Does anyone know what time it is?   36
He's sociable, and very secure   37

3-Me'n'Norm

She would rather be lucky than good   41
The best umbrellas are the one's that are lost   42
This bath is for the birds   44
More than one way to get burned at the beach   45
There's always something cooking at our house   46
The hurrier I go . . . oh, stick it in your ear   48
What would we carry in a gun rack?   49
Two little kids, one old grouch   51
Forget wallpaper, slap on some paint   52
Water, water everywhere it isn't supposed to be   54

4-Eat, drink and . . .

Winter is best for gardening 57
Come on, garden, do your thing 58
Culture shock in the supermarket 60
Report card time on a summer's work 61
The man knows good food 63
Vidalia onions: The rest of the story 64
Tomatoes: Red, yellow, green and fried 66
What's for supper? Fry a mess of greens 68

5-The media

We're weirding our language 71
A fond farewell to USA YESTERDAY 72
It takes a whiner to know a whiner 74
From ashes . . . to ducks? 75
'Eyes have it, no, the 'Ears recover 77
Lewis and Lucy and the good old days 78
Far too many TV miniseries 80
I can't remember what I forgot 82

6-On the road again

Four wheels or I'm walking 85
Butterflies and other migrants 86
Just hangin' out on Saturday night 88
These oranges left a sour taste 89
Getting there in plenty of time 91
Dream vacation was only a dream 92
The real reason people stay in motels 94

7-This is progress?

Wanted: Small all-purpose opener 97
No wife means no phone ringing 98
Number, please? All 35 or 36 of them 100
Tax time causes ringing in ear 101
Evening of TV made to order 103
Some assembly may be required 104
That silly rabbit let us down 105
It's time to switch to paper plates 107
Bad things happen to good people 108
What will they think of next? 110

8-Potpourri

'You can have a whole pie by yourself' 113
Searching for a class on how to schedule classes 115
A little of this, a little of that 116
Simple wedding, but what a reception! 117
Terrible Tony and the pink flamingo caper 119
All that money, but where's Ed? 120
One man's junk, another's treasure 121
In search of a plain, brown wrapper 123
Really, I don't want the right oppurtunity 124
You know what makes me mad? WHACK! 126
Fine for littering . . . just try it 127
Junk to you, memories for me 129
Birds and bugs and X-rated stuff 131

9-High fashion

My ties' statement: We're terribly out of date 134
OK, who stole my pants pockets? 135
Shelby knot joins the hangman's noose 136
If the shoe fits, put an ad on it 138

10-Season-ing

A severe case of cabin fever 141
Weathering the storms 142
Rain brings flood of bad news 144
Time to enjoy summer daze 146
Help me, I'm falling 147
Another September, another birthday 148

11-Life with father

Dad got a kick out of his short life 152
First and 10, do it again 153
Rollin' a smoke in the days B.C. 155
An early switch or a caning later? 156

12-To your health!

No ifs, and or butts about it 160
Medical advice: Don't read the studies 161

Take two and call me in the morning   162
Mr. Coffee loses his Mrs. Olson   164
Looking for the Smith Brothers   166
The A,B,C's of health care   167
One of God's special children   169

13-Happy holidaze

Two Christmas gifts we are happy without   172
I can change my mind . . . and my shorts, too   173
For whom the Christmases toll   175
'Dear Santa, About that train' . . .   176
You have to do it by the book   178
Go soak a noodle, Ann   179
What goes up must come down   181
Let there be lights until spring   182
Resolved: Check this a year later   184
Happy birthday to all of U.S.!   185
Thankful this day only comes once a year   187

14- -30-

A teacher who taught me a lasting lesson   190
Lewis is dead and I feel rotten   191
A newspaperman's newspaperman   193
The most learned man I ever knew   195
Erma knew how to humor us   197

1-Fun and games

You never get too old
to have heroes. And the best
places to look for them are
movies, TV or on the playing
fields. On second thought,
maybe not. Some of my biggest
heroes are just other folks.

Where have all all our heroes gone?

Hero—1. **a**: A mythological or legendary figure often of divine descent endowed with great strength or ability **b**: an illustrious warrior **c**: a man admired for his achievements and noble qualities **d**: one that shows great courage

Have you noticed that the hero population seems to be declining? It appears that way. Hero could be added to the endangered species list any day now. The next step would be to begin repopulation efforts, such as is being done with buffaloes and even wolves. It wouldn't be an easy task. You have to find some of the dwindling species first, then relocate it and hope that it will multiply.

Oh, sure, there are plenty of heroes if you use definition **d** above. Not a day goes by that we don't see, hear or read about the courageous efforts of those who are willing to put their lives on the line to help others. But we don't hear a whole lot about **a** types except in books or movies, and the **b**'s only in wars.

There are a few **c** heroes around, but very few. They're the ones going the way of the buffalo and the wolf.

It wasn't always that way. A half century ago, heroes were plentiful. At least in the world of my boyhood. For starters, anyone wearing a Cincinnati Reds uniform in the late 1930s or early '40s qualified. Bucky Walters and Paul Derringer were the greatest. But don't forget Ernie Lombardi. Or Frank McCormick and Johnny Vander Meer. Good thing Marge Schott didn't have to pay the 1940 Reds 1990s salaries.

Roy Rogers was an early hero, too. I wasn't even old enough or smart enough to know he was a Scioto County boy when he first appeared in the movies. But it didn't make any difference, because Roy could ride and rope and always did the right thing. Later, when I learned he was a home boy, he was an even bigger hero.

There were even heroes in our neighborhood. One was a pharmacist named Eldon Smith, a big, friendly man who could always take time out from behind the counter to talk about baseball. He also took his son and me to the church's father and son banquet. First banquet I ever attended. Another hero, whom I won't name because he would be embarrassed, was the brightest star on the high school football and basketball teams. We kids would even try to walk like he did.

Somewhere along the line, though, the world started looking for heroes in a different light. We measured them by different standards, and it became more difficult to be a hero then. Presidents used to be heroes. It came with the job. Everyone looked up to the president. Not anymore. We started looking at them a little more closely and found they didn't quite measure up. Once we began checking closely for faults, we found that

6

many of those we once saw as heroes have the same flaws we do. Often more.

We want our heroes to be honest, good looking, personable, intelligent, hard working, courageous and even more. We set pretty high standards for our role models. We were looking for someone just a tad short of perfect. Very few people passed this tougher test.

Many of us elevated baseball star Cal Ripken Jr. to a hero's pedestal last summer when he set a record for the most consecutive games played. Ripken was indeed a breath of fresh air in a sports world populated mostly by oversized and overpaid prima donnas who want a fee before they'll give a kid an autograph. But Ripken himself would be the first to tell you he simply was doing what millions of people do every day—performing the job he's paid to do.

Television must take most of the blame for making so many of us anti-hero. It caused us to confuse celebrity with heroism. When you look closely, they're rarely synonymous.

There's another dictionary definition of a hero: submarine. Then you look under submarine and find, in addition to an underwater vessel, that it's a large sandwich with a variety of fillings such as cheese, cold cuts—including baloney—lettuce tomatoes etc. That is what so many of today's would-be heroes are—filled with baloney.

January, 1996

Kathie Lee is a Super singer

OK, Super Bowl XXIX was a real stinkeroo. So what else is new? Twelve of the last 15 have required fumigation of the stadium. Surely, we're getting used to it by now. Besides, as the old saying goes, it doesn't matter if you win or lose, it's what happens before the game, at halftime and during what seemed like thousands of commercial time-outs.

Where else could you have spent a Sunday evening watching a chubby-cheeked youngster sucking on a straw with sufficient vigor to pull himself right into a Pepsi bottle? Or out-of-work governors Mario Cuomo and Ann Richards huckstering Doritos? That's class. Real class. But the true stars of the day were Steve Young and Kathie Lee Gifford.

If you don't know what Steve Young did by now, obviously you couldn't care less. If you do care, dig last Sunday's sports section out of the garbage can, recycling bin or bird cage, shake off the coffee grounds or whatever and read it for yourself.

I'd rather talk about Kathie Lee. Steve Young is good, all right. He can pass and he can run. As far as I know, Kathie Lee can do neither.

But Kathie Lee is much prettier than Steve. And she can

sing. Oh, man, can she ever!

I'm here to tell you that Kathie Lee just plumb sang the daylights out of "The Star Spangled Banner" just prior to kickoff. By the time I had quit applauding, the 49ers had a 14-0 lead.

Kathie Lee sang our National Anthem the way it's supposed to be sung. She sang it in the traditional way. She sang it with clarity, with enthusiasm, with feeling. And she sang it with love. I could mention her pure tone, dynamics, interpretation, emphasis and the slight pause before a crescendo finish. But those are all music terms and I have no idea in the world what they mean.

I guess what I'm trying to say is that Kathie Lee sang "The Star Spangled Banner" the way Miss Walden tried to teach us tone-deaf and near musical illiterate kids at Harding School back in the '40s.

Never mind that there was some controversy over whether it would be Kathie Lee or Barbra Streisand singing our song at this year's Super Bore. More than likely, Ms. Streisand would have done a good job. Mrs. Gifford did a great job.

Not all that many singers handle the National Anthem that well. Kelsey Grammer did a few nights later on David Letterman's show. You know Grammer, the guy who plays psychiatrist "Frasier" on his show of the same name as well as on "Cheers" a few years ago. I never did understand why Grammer was singing the "Star Spangled Banner" at midnight for Letterman. But he did, and quite well, thank you.

The song isn't always treated as kindly.

Whitney Houston sang it at a Super Bowl a couple of years ago. I like Whitney Houston. I play her tapes and CDs frequently. I really like them. But her job on the National Anthem didn't turn me on. The crowd in the stadium went bonkers. But I think it was more because of who she was than what she had just done.

For some reason, singers can't accept the song the way Francis Scott Key wrote it. They have to jazz it up or add all sorts of gimmicks. What they really do is screw it up.

One of the first was Jose Feliciano at either a World Series or All-Star Game in Detroit some time ago. That was the first time I recall boos during or after the National Anthem.

And can anyone ever forget Roseanne (Barr? Arnold? Whatever) at a baseball game in San Diego a few years back? When she punctuated her butchering of the song by grabbing her crotch, a la Michael Jackson?

Thank you, Kathie Lee, for a beautiful job. If you take requests, I have one: Please see if you can give husband Frank a personality/enthusiasm transfusion or transplant.

February, 1995

Roy still reigns as King of the Cowboys

It was the 1940s all over again.

It was the Stanley Theater in Sciotoville, where I grew up, and, later, the Garden on Chillicothe Street in Portsmouth, where I ventured as a teen-ager. It was the good guys against the bad guys, and in those days, the good guys always won.

And, as everyone in these parts knows, the best of the good guys was the King of the Cowboys, Scioto County's own Roy Rogers.

He could ride, he could rope. He could shoot and he could use his fists. He took his lumps now and then, but that usually happened only when some lowdown sidewinder slipped in a sucker punch.

Roy Rogers always won in the end, though, and then you discovered he could sing, too, almost as well as he could pile up the bad guys in the nearest watering trough. When he rode off into the sunset on the familiar "Happy Trails," many of the young cowpokes in the audience were ready to sit through a double feature again for the same happy ending.

The King of the Cowboys came home the first weekend in June for the sixth annual Roy Rogers Festival. The script was as well written as for any of his movies in a career that began with "Under Western Stars" back in 1938. The man in the tall white hat was cheered at his every appearance.

There was a rodeo, as well as a golf scramble tournament. But the real highlights were a downtown parade and a grand finale banquet. The latter drew approximately 500 Roy Rogers faithful, so many more than were expected that the start of serving was delayed.

They had come to see and honor a man many had never seen before, even in the movies. They don't make his kind anymore.

For newcomers to Southern Ohio, or the young (which includes just about anyone under 40), one of the best places to get acquainted with Roy Rogers is at Bureau of Motor Vehicles office on Fifth Street.

Registrar Don Gordley, who also is president of Portsmouth Area Community Exhibits, has what surely must be the largest collection of Rogers memorabilia in the cowboy star's hometown. Some of it, he owns; the rest has been donated or is on loan.

There are movie posters, comic books, coloring books and the oldtime big-little books so many of us grew up reading from cover to cover and over and over.

There are limited-edition plates, play money dollar bills with Rogers' face instead of George Washington's and two paintings of his boyhood home on Duck Run, one painted in 1953, the other in 1982.

9

There are records and sheet music and much, much more. And right in the middle is the familiar white hat, symbol of all that is good . . . the symbol of Roy Rogers.

And, of course, don't forget his faithful horse, Trigger. All nine of the large movie posters identify Rogers as King of the Cowboys; all but one of them salute Trigger as the Smartest Horse in the movies.

The 77 years that have passed since Rogers was born as Leonard Slye in Cincinnati—right about where Riverfront Stadium is now—have been good to him.

Maybe it was the good country living after the Slyes moved off their Ohio River houseboat and out to the farm. Or it could have been the good life of 43 years of marriage to the Sweetheart of the West, Dale Evans.

At any rate, Roy looked fit enough to tangle with any varmint who attempted to rustle the herd or connive to steal the ranch. And don't bet that he wouldn't win, just as he always did.

There was only one slight twinge of regret during this entire salute to the King of the Cowboys. We had to share Roy Rogers with all of his hometown, his family, all of his fans. Back in the good old days, in the movie houses long since closed, it was just the two of us, riding side by side, both wearing white hats. And we whupped the bad guys every time.

June, 1989

Namesake of a legend

If his wife hadn't taken so long shampooing, drying and doing her hair, we probably never would have met Roy Rogers Ross Jr.

He was leaning against his car, parked in front of the bath house at Ft. Boonesborough State Park near Lexington, Ky. We were with two grandchildren at our camp site about 50 yards away.

Roy Rogers Ross Jr. became weary of waiting for the final curl to be put into place and began walking toward the two playing youngsters and their coffee-sipping baby sitters.

It was a beautiful day in late October—tailor made for the four-day weekend Roy and Shelby Ross had in mind when they gathered their camping gear and headed out from Raleigh, N.C. There was an old mine—or some other tourist attraction; I don't remember exactly what—they wanted to see in Stearns, Ky.

They also wanted to go to the Kentucky Horse Park just north of Lexington, then spend a night at Ft. Boonesborough.

Now it was Monday morning, the tent was down, folded and packed away in the car and RRR Jr. was ready to head home and go back to work the next day as a Raleigh fireman. As soon as Shelby finished putting on her traveling face.

Roy Rogers Ross Jr. is a friendly young man—probably still on the low side of 30—and easy to get acquainted with. He introduced himself and when we told him we were from the cowboy star's hometown, he knew what we were talking about: Portsmouth and Duck Run, across the river in Ohio.

No, he said, he had never been there—no closer than where we were at the time. And, no, he wasn't named after Roy Rogers.

"But my Dad was," he added quickly. "I was named after my Dad."

He recalls—or at least hearing about—a trip to California and having his picture taken seated on Dale Evans' lap.

Roy, however, was up on the roof doing some repairs to the barn and that was as close as Roy Rogers Ross Jr. ever came to seeing cowboy Roy Rogers.

The following night we were in Gatlinburg, Tenn., and, if all had gone well, Roy Rogers Ross Jr. was home in North Carolina getting ready to go back to the firehouse.

But that wasn't all we were to see of Roy Rogers. You can spend only so much time—and money—in discount malls, so we turned to antique shops where the prices were even higher.

The piece de resistance there was a grapevine wreath saluting our very own King of the Cowboys. Perhaps it wasn't exactly what you would want hanging over the living room fireplace. But it certainly would have made a fine conversation piece. Wound around the grapevine circle was an aged, brown wool scarf that probably had been very pretty—as well as very warm—in its day.

"Probably valuable," commented a woman gazing at it. She looked more like a browser than a clerk, so we nodded in agreement.

Also attached to the wreath were a:

Roy Rogers neckerchief. But it was black. Cowboy good guys wear white and everyone knows Roy was always a good guy. Still is.

Postcard size picture of you know who.

Little cap pistol.

Bit of old-timey days movie film.

Pocket knife.

Horseshoe pin.

Brightly colored American flag pin.

But there was no price tag to be seen. What's that old saying? Something about if you have to ask how much, you probably can't afford it. Probably not.

March, 1993

9 holes a year, that's par for me

Perhaps it was just a coincidence.

One minute, or at least that's the way it seemed to me, I was scanning the sports page and stumbled upon a story about a golf tournament. It was on the last page of the section, back where a golfer might refer to it as the deep rough.

I didn't recognize a single name in the story. Bobby Wadkins and Mark Brooks were engaging in a wonderful duel, the sports writer said.

Bobby Who? Mark What? I said, to no one in particular. Then, turning to the page where all the teensy, tiny type is, I scanned the listing of the top 13 scorers (space was tight today). Behind Wadkins and What'shisname were 11 other strangers.

Maybe this was a tennis tournament instead. No, even though the word "golf" was nowhere to be seen, there was sufficient mention of "par," "birdie," "bogey," "PGA" and "$1.3 million" that it was obvious the reporter was writing about golf.

But where were Jack, Arnie and Gary? Oh, that's right—they're on the senior tour now with Chi Chi. But how about Greg Norman, Ben Crenshaw, that other kid from Ohio State, what's his name? John Cook, I think it is. They're still playing, aren't they? And Ballesteros, or however it's spelled, Chip Beck, Tom Kite, Corey Pavin, Craig Stadler . . .

My Lord, don't tell me another whole generation is over the hill and on the way to the senior tees!

Anyway, less than 24 hours later I found myself teeing up a ball for my annual round of golf. The other three were pretty good golfers. They're the kind who can talk about being on the green in 2 or 3; I think about it in terms such as being on the green by 4 or 5:30, or before dark at the latest.

It's hard to remember all the important things you're supposed to do: Keep your head down, stomach in (Hah! That'll be the day), shoulders square, eyes open, stuff like that.

Actually, I hadn't even dressed properly to begin with.

"You're going to wear shorts, aren't you?" asked the woman who always snickers at my backswing, follow through, back porch swing and any other part of my game.

Heck, no, I answered. My second, third, fourth and all other shots until I finally reach the green are in deep rough. There are briars and brambles and hard telling what else that just have a magnetic-like pull on my ball. There might even be snakes. I can't go in there bare legged.

My golfing partners all showed up in shorts. At least, I think they were wearing shorts. I don't usually make a habit of looking at other men's legs and there weren't any women on the course.

Wonder of wonders, I hit a pretty good tee shot off No. 1. For me, it was a great shot. And compared with my partners' drives, it was darn good. I would have laughed out loud, but I knew what was ahead.

Thirty or 40 minutes later, I inquired what was par for this nine-hole layout.

"Thirty-six," replied one who is a club member.

Great, I told them. I'm one under, so I'm heading for the clubhouse.

It didn't work. We had completed only four holes and they threatened to run over me with a golf cart if I didn't finish the round.

I didn't do too badly. I was two shots better than Bobby Wadkins' 65 that had put him into the lead going into the final round of the Kemper Open. Of course, he had played 18 holes and I only half that many.

I have no idea how Wadkins finished in his tournament. I do know, however, that if he didn't fall flat on his face or do something equally disastrous, he took home a lot of dollars. He'll be back out on a golf course somewhere this weekend, next weekend, the weekend after that and so on.

Not me, buddy. I've played my nine for this summer. That's par for me, the only one I'll ever get. See you guys in '95.

June, 1994

The big ones always get away

This is a fish story.

You know what that means, don't you? Exaggerations. Half-truths. Fibs. Out-and-out lies. It's your job to decide which is which.

Fish stories are something new for me. I've never written any before and have told very few for one simple reason: I never have fished much. In fact, I've had only three fishing licenses in my entire life.

The first was back in the really early '60s when three small children lived at our house. For some reason no one ever explained to me, small children like to fish. They don't like to dig worms, nor do they like to pick worms up and put them on a fish hook. They don't know what to do when they catch a fish except jump up and down and shout. Neither do I.

After those three small children grew up and moved on to more exciting activities, I didn't have another fishing license until about 25 years later. That was after we had moved to Alabama where people like to catch fish, fry them and eat them with hush puppies. Some even jump up and down and shout.

I woke up one Christmas morning and found that I had been

13

surprised with a new rod and reel, a tackle box and more hooks, line and sinkers than I would ever know what to do with. Ten days later, I suffered a heart attack (probably because I was so thrilled with my gift) and didn't get around to acquiring another fishing license for several months.

The third and final, license was bought just a few weeks ago. Why not? After all, that rod and reel and all the accompanying paraphernalia are as good as brand new, I was advised. Either use it or put it in a yard sale. I'd much rather go to yard sales than have one; it would be simpler to use the fishing gear than sell it.

A camping trip to Alum Creek State Park, just north of Columbus, Ohio, had been in the works for several months and would provide a wonderful opportunity.

There were many fishermen—and fisherwomen, too—trying their luck. Most of them, however, were in boats. I wasn't. I can't hold on to a boat and still handle a rod and reel. I settled instead for a shady spot on the bank in a secluded little inlet near the campground.

Bluegills were biting, I had been told at the bait shop. Good, I replied with the confidence of a veteran angler who was going to fill his stringer and go back to the camper for a supper of fried fish.

I had no intention at all of putting any fish on a stringer. I hoped to catch a few, of course, but I was going to reel them in, look at them with pride, then throw them back in . . . just like the pros on TV.

I pulled in seven that were big enough to be keepers, plus one striped bass that was several inches shorter than the minimum. I think it was a bass. It could have been a tenor or baritone, for all I know about fish. It had been a good day, I said to myself as I started back to the campground.

But I came to a spot that was so inviting. It was shady and even had a fallen log for me to sit on. I just had to throw out a line one more time. That's when my fish story happened. I hadn't even been watching and something had taken my hook. Now it was trying to take my rod. I wasn't ready for this. I just catch bluegills and crappies about the size of my hand; I don't know what to do with a fish that bends my fishing rod until it looks like this?

I had no idea what it was. The only fish I'm well acquainted with is tuna. I open a can occasionally. Sardines, too, and maybe some salmon or mackerel. The one on my line wasn't in a can; I wish it had been.

What I had caught was the biggest, ugliest and meanest catfish I had ever seen. I guessed him to be 18 to 24 inches long and about three pounds. Allowing for the lying that goes with the sport, he had to be at least 15 to 18 inches long.

I didn't want to tangle with him. Those ugly whiskers that I feared could sting me were intimidating. I also had been told there were fins that could mess up your fingers if you didn't know what you were doing. I didn't. Know, that is. While I stood there wondering what to do, that wily old cat gave one last flip, snapped the line and swam away, hook still in his mouth, sinker hanging out of it.

I trudged back to the RV empty handed.

Not long before dusk, I decided to go back to the old fishing hole.

I loaded up another hook with the fattest earthworm I could find and threw my line as close as possible to where the big one got away . . . just a few feet from a fallen tree that was surrounded by a few limbs.

You already are 'way ahead of me, aren't you? You've guessed what happened!

I pulled in that very same catfish with my first hook still in his mouth and the sinker dangling nearby, right?

Of course not! To tell the truth—and that's what I'm doing—I didn't get another nibble the rest of the evening.

July, 1994

The Wonders of basketball

Even though December has bowed out in favor of January and 1992 has surrendered to '93, let me tell you about one of my Christmas gifts.

Not all of them; I don't want to bore you. Besides, I didn't get that many.

But one in particular stood out from all the others.

It was a book, one of eight I was rewarded with, including a new dictionary that includes words I have used before but will never find their way into a family newspaper. I hope.

This particular book is an oldie: "The Fabulous Waterloo Wonders," written in 1961 by Dick Burdette.

Burdette is a 1953 graduate of Portsmouth High School in the area where I grew up. He later spent a year and a half at the Daily Times in Portsmouth as a general assignment reporter—writing obits, features etc.—and taught in Scioto County schools. I was his city editor at the newspaper.

Dick later taught journalism at Bowling Green and Colorado State universities and worked for newspapers in Findlay, Ohio, and Fort Collins, Colo., plus 12 years at the Orlando Sentinel in Florida.

Six years ago, Burdette moved to Lexington, Ky., and began writing a column for the Herald-Leader. I read him every time I get to the local public library and steal from his columns as often as I can.

Last summer, I began dropping broadside hints to my elder daughter—who lives in Lexington and writes for the Richmond Register—that Burdette's book would make a wonderful gift. For me, of course.

She'll forget, I told myself. But if she does, I'll just keep hinting. She didn't forget.

It was no easy task. The book, which originally sold for $2, is no longer available in stores. She had to track down the author and talk him out of one of his few remaining copies.

When I opened the small package wrapped in the funny-looking paper, no one else in the room even knew where Waterloo is (it's in rural Lawrence County, about 20 miles north of Ironton) or who the Wonders were. Fame is fleeting.

Actually, mention of the Waterloo Wonders will usually bring one of three reactions: blank stares such as my gift book prompted; genuine enthusiasm from those who played against, watched or read about the Wonders when they won state championships in 1934 and '35 or wonderful lies from phonies who say they saw them play time and again but really weren't even born yet.

Burdette's interest in the Waterloo Wonders was stirred when, as a youngster in grade school, he would frequently ride with his dad, Jack, on the elder Burdette's Portsmouth Cake & Cookie route up through Wheelersburg and over into Superior, Pine Grove, Pedro and other wide spots in Lawrence County roads.

He would see road signs pointing to Waterloo and he knew that was the home of the Wonders. But there was never time to go there because Jack had to deliver those cakes and cookies while they were still fresh.

In 1959, the 25th anniversary of the Wonders' state championship, Burdette suggested to the late Fritz Howell, Associated Press sports editor for Ohio, that the team be recognized at the state tournament.

After the ceremony and while listening to the former schoolboy stars spin tales of their exploits—they had a 42-3 regular season record in 1934-35—Burdette thought to himself: "This ought to be put on paper." And he did.

He talked to the former players, their coach and school officials in an effort to separate fact from fiction. He dug into old newspaper files and picture albums.

When he was finished, Burdette had compiled the only chronicle of what is perhaps Ohio's most colorful, successful and even controversial high school basketball team. It includes team pictures, scores of a hundred or more games and newspaper accounts of season highlights.

It also was my favorite Christmas gift of 1992, a gift from an old friend and co-worker as well as from my daughter.

16

P.S.: Please don't ask to borrow it. I'd hate to say no and I don't want to make up some cock-and-bull story about having a waiting list that extends into 2003.

January, 1993

Forget luge, go for a snooze

Please, don't think I'm not patriotic. I am. I can, and do, wave the flag every chance I get, even though our pole is bare right now. Wintry winds tattered our flag too badly to leave it up any longer. And the roads have been too icy to go shopping for a new one.

I want to get the patriotism issue settled so it won't be questioned when I tell you I don't give a big rat's patootie about the upcoming Winter Olympics. To tell the truth, I don't know when they start or where.

The only thing I want to know is when they'll be over and regular television programming will be resumed. Then, perhaps, we'll get to see some real winter sports such as basketball and ice hockey, which run from about the first of October until sometime in June; football, which ended its season the first week in February, and baseball, which begins spring training in just a few days and will end about the time many of us are thinking about Thanksgiving and the start of Christmas shopping. Or is that when we're supposed to finish Christmas shopping? Whatever.

Anyway, except for the possible exception of ice hockey—which really is boxing and wrestling on skates while carrying funny-looking baseball bats—the Winter Olympics are strange.

They do things called the luge and the giant slalom. They do Alpine skiing and Nordic skiing and most of us don't know the difference. Do we? Of course not. That's why the winners always are from places such as Norway, Finland or Liechtenstein and have names like Wolfgang, Erich and Heidi.

You know why? Because where these people live, it's snowing when they're born and it snows until they die. That's why they're always wearing skates, skis or snowshoes.

Our athletes are named Michael, Bo, Suzy and Monica. They wear Nikes, Reeboks and Adidas. And they play on dirt, grass and Astroturf. Or under a dome.

Ice? That belongs only in a glass.

If you want real Winter Olympics, come up with something like the 10-minute doze or the 30-minute snooze. That's more like it. For those more competitive, many of us have been practicing for weeks on such events as the six-step fall and the 10-yard sprawl.

If those are too pedestrian, we can climb into our vehicles and practice the four-wheel spin and the 25-yard skid. The more reckless of us sometimes advance to the two-car bumper-thumper or even the 10-car pile-up. The latter is kind of like a relay race in which you exchange names of insurance companies instead of a baton.

The main reason so many of us can't really get into these Winter Olympics is because of the scoring. In a basketball game, you know it's the team that is scoring more points. In the mile run, it's the runner out in front of the pack. In the shot put, it's the one who grunts the loudest and throws that steel ball the farthest.

It's a whole different ball game in things such as figure skating. You never know who is winning or why. Sometimes you have a pretty good idea that someone is losing because he or she messed up and went sliding across the ice on his or her butt instead of skates.

How do they judge these things? Do they get points for skimpiest costumes? Biggest smiles? Loudest applause? Beats me.

And speaking of beating, how about this Nancy Kerrigan-Tonya Harding thing! Hey, I'd have to be Arnold Schwarzenegger to touch that nasty little incident with a 10-foot pole.

Instead, I'd use it to become a pole vaulter. Now that's another sport in which you can tell who the winner is: the one who vaults the highest over a bar way up in the air without knocking the bar down.

And there is no snow or ice involved. Not a flake or an icicle.

February, 1994

Hunters, don't forget to take your lunch

Hunters bagged more than 2,000 deer in the county where I live and the one next to it during the recently completed gun season.

I wasn't among them, for two very good reasons: I don't own a gun and I didn't have a license.

Bow season continues through January, I'm told, and there also will be a three-day primitive weapon season. I don't own a bow and don't have any primitive weapons, either, unless big sticks count.

So it doesn't appear that I'll be able to tell any first-person deer-hunting stories again this year. But I do know a pretty good hunter who also is a master at story telling. His name is Don James, a retired state veterinarian, who lives out in the country just a few miles from my home. It isn't real clear to me what a state veterinarian does; he probably treated animals and gave them shots. That figures, because but Don James is pretty good at shooting the bull. Judge for yourself. This is his story:

"Over the years, deer hunting has provided me with a lot of pleasure. In fact, it's been one of the most enjoyable outdoor activities that I've engaged in. I've shared this feeling of deer hunting with my Dad and later, as my own two sons became big enough to go with me, and a host of friends. I've accumulated a lifetime of good memories related to deer hunting and it seems that all those experiences have been shared with others.

"Except one time, and let me tell you about that hunt.

"I went by myself on one occasion, the only occasion that I can remember going alone, and various things led to that. My friend, John, whom I have hunted with for years, had sickness in the family and couldn't go. My two sons had to work and couldn't get off. My neighbor, Bill, was sick and couldn't go and I almost talked myself out of going. But at the last moment I decided to go ahead, even if I had to hunt by myself.

"I hunted in Jackson County that year and drove up there in the truck and got out and it was a gloomy morning. I usually hunt all day if I'm not successful before the day's over, stay out till quitting time, take a lunch with me. As I was getting my gear out of the truck, I discovered that I'd forgotten my lunch which I'd prepared at home and left on the counter top. I did have some dried apples with me so I filled my pockets with dried apples and thought that would suffice.

"As I started back through the woods toward the top of the hill, it began to rain, only slightly at first but by the time I'd gotten back to where I intended to hunt, it was raining pretty hard. So I looked for a leaning tree or a rock cliff or something where I could get in out of the rain. I wasn't successful in finding anything like that, but about 50 yards away I saw a large chestnut log. I walked over there and the log was hollow and I thought it was raining so hard I'd just crawl into that log and perhaps the rain would slacken later. And this I did.

"I'd been in there a good while, quite comfortable, even dozed a little. After a while the rain did slacken and I thought well, it's going to quit, I'll get out and to my amazement, those dried apples that I'd put into my pockets had become wet and had swollen and I was wedged in that log! Tightly! I couldn't move. I couldn't even squirm.

"I panicked momentarily, I guess. Way back on the hill by myself, no one knew where I was. I thought, I'm going to die, right back here on this hill in this log. No one would ever find me. I suppose most of you have experienced or heard of people who have had near-death experiences and had visions of things in their past that came before their eyes, very vividly. That actually happens. It happened to me.

"I remembered several events from years back. I even

19

remembered that one time I voted for a Democrat. And I felt so small that I slid out of that log and here I am today, ready to hunt again."

P.S.: This is a nonpartisan, nonpolitical column. Democrats may insert Republican in the paragraph above and everyone can live happily ever after.

December, 1993

XXVII reasons to skip the game

At last! Today is the BIG day. This is the one everyone has been awaiting.

At least, that's what everyone has been telling us. Particularly in the last two weeks.

There is no way you possibly could have missed all the hype leading up to a certain football game that will dominate the tube this afternoon and evening.

For that reason, the S word and the B word have been banished from what you are now reading. Instead of SB, which many non-fans too easily could turn into a string of SOBs aimed at TV sets everywhere, let's simply refer to today's event as XXVII.

And by the way, isn't that about the stupidest way of numbering games you ever saw? You never hear of anyone paying $M for a ticket or a quarterback throwing a XLI-yard pass for a touchdown. So why is this the XXVIIth you-know-what?

But no more about that. Instead, what you are being offered here are alternatives to XXVII. You don't have to have a VI- or an VIII-pack and spend III hours or more watching another in a long line of mismatches.

Choose something from among the following:

I. Don't you think Jan. XXXI is about time to get the outside Christmas lights down? Sure it is. And when they're untangled and packed away for another XII months, it might not be a bad idea to get that tree out of the living room. Either take it down or pull the drapes.

II. Too cold to work outside on the lights? It's raining and you're afraid to play with electricity? Read a book. Some of you probably haven't read a book since a high school literature class. Don't plunge into anything recklessly; choose something with a lot of pictures, then work into the words gradually.

III. Hey, how about a movie! You can even take the kids, providing you can work out a second or third mortgage on the house.

IV. But maybe it's too pretty of a day to stay inside. Take a drive. About 50 miles would be about right. There's a very good

20

reason for this: Usually, the farther you get from home, the cheaper gasoline is.

V. If you prefer something more constructive, stay home and work on your Roman numerals. Forty years from now, how many of your friends will know they're watching LXVII? Hey, how many of them will still be alive?

VI. This would be a good day to work on your address book and update your Christmas card list. It surely needs it. What else would explain why we received fewer this year?

VII. Some of you may want to seek out a dance studio or a gym and sign up for a class in acrobatics. Every sign points toward a surge in the popularity of flip-flops. It's already big in Arkansas and Washington and likely will be coming to your neighborhood soon.

This was started as a project that would give you XXVII alternatives to watching Game XXVII today. But space limitations have trimmed it by XX.

But if you choose wisely and budget your time carefully, you should get finished in time for a VI o'clock kickoff. It probably will be V or X minutes later; they never start right on the hour because of commercials that make the networks M, V, X and even Cs of dollars.

I'll see you on the XL-yard line.

January, 1993

One strike ends, time for another

"Baseball strike ends."

That's what the headline said in the newspaper I read the other day. The newspaper you read said pretty much the same thing, no doubt. But headlines don't always tell the complete story. They can't, because of space limitations. The headline writer had only so much space in which to fit only so many words and did the best he (or she) could.

If the headline had been a column longer, the person whose job it is to try to capsulize an entire story into just a few words might have added two more: "for now."

Because the longest work stoppage ever in sports could break out again at any time. There's no guarantee the delayed 1995 season will begin on its new April 26 opening day. Or that it won't end around the mid-season All-Star Game, as was expected last season.

The late-starting 1995 season could end on Aug. 12, the first anniversary of the beginning of the strike whose end was reported under the headline cited above. The players' union might instead choose to hang up their gloves on the eve of the World Series, which would hit Major League Baseball and team

21

owners right where it hurts the most.

Can you spell c-h-e-c-k-b-o-o-k?

Any of these scenarios are possible. They're possible because that headline said "Baseball strike ends." It didn't say "Baseball strike settled." There's a huge difference.

Absolutely nothing was settled. The owners simply crumpled in the face of a National Labor Relations Board ruling and a federal court decision to let the games begin under terms of the expired contract that led to last year's strike. The expected lockout by owners never came about because such an action could have resulted in sizeable fines. Even millionaires can lose only so many dollars—whether they be owners or players.

By the way, was the NLRB really intended for cases such as this? When it originally was established, did anyone really think men earning millions for playing a game would be seeking NLRB assistance? Or was it set up to provide relief for oppressed working men and women? Do those whose average annual salary is $1.2 million—some of whom are in the $8-million neighborhood—actually consider themselves to be working men?

Just wondering.

OK, so the baseball strike has ended. Not settled, mind you, but ended. What are we, the fans of what mistakenly is referred to as the National Pastime, going to do about it?

Are we going to storm the ticket office of our local Major League team and fork over two or three times as many dollars than they're worth for tickets to see a bunch of millionaires play a game? And as much for a hot dog, box of popcorn and something to drink as we'd pay for the blue-plate special at a hometown restaurant?

Are we going to let our kids pay astronomical prices for shirts, caps, even entire baseball uniforms? And $15 to $20 or $25 or more for an already wealthy man's autograph that can't even be read once the ink is dry?

Are we going to sit in front of the TV until our eyes bug out, watching the boys of summer and hurrying out afterward to buy products of the sponsors?

You know we will. At the very least, far too many of us will.

What a pity!

What we should do is go on a 232-day strike of our own. Major League Baseball, owners and players alike, told us to go to hell last August. Let's send them the same message this April. We got along fine without them last summer and fall; we can do it again this year for an entire season.

We can go out to the ball diamond and watch a high school or college team play for the love of the game, not for lots of $$$$$. Later on, the minor leaguers—including our own Explorers—will suit up. They play for pay, but very little of it.

And there will be Junior Legion baseball and plenty of kids' games—Little League, Knothole, whatever it's called where you live.

As for Major League Baseball, let it find replacement fans.

April, 1995

2-D.C.(entralize it)

Holidays, postage stamps,

counting noses, even setting

clocks . . . our almighty

government has a very big

hand in it all.

George and Abe deserve better

The first celebration of George Washington's birthday as a holiday is believed to have taken place in 1745.

It was a particularly fine day in Westmoreland County, Va., and, having just become a teen-ager, George felt there were far more interesting things to do than spend the day in school. George's favorite subject was American history. The curriculum committee, however, hadn't come up with such a course yet. He later would become fond of mathematics, but not until someone had invented the calculator.

So George did what any other teen-age boy would have done. He played hooky.

George wasn't a member of a youth gang. There weren't any malls near his home and even if there had been, he wasn't old enough to get a driver's license. Cruising the mall was out.

About all there was left for George to do was stay out of sight in case the truant officer was on the prowl. And above all, he mustn't let himself get caught by Mom and Pop Washington. He succeeded, the day passed quickly and George enjoyed it immensely.

But trouble was awaiting him at the dinner table.

"Well, George," Pop Washington addressed him. "How was your day? What did you do in school?"

"I cannot tell a lie," replied the crestfallen George. "I didn't go to school today. I played hooky. And that's not the half of it. I also cut down your cherry tree."

Pop Washington could hardly believe his ears. He was so impressed with his son's honesty he immediately sent a fax to his good friend Newton Gingrich in Georgia telling what the boy had done and asking if Newt, as he was known to his friends and enemies alike, could help get George into politics.

If you ever have listened to Paul Harvey, you surely know the rest of the story so there is no need to repeat it here. Suffice it to say that is why we celebrated George's birthday last Monday with humongous sales and a day off work for anyone even remotely connected with government.

Initially, the holiday was known as George Washington's Birthday, although the young scalawags who revered the hooky-playing George are known to have referred to it as George Birthington's Wash Day. For shame!

But as time passed, the holiday was moved from George's Feb. 22 date of birth, combined with Abe Lincoln's Feb. 12 and put on the calendar as the third Monday in February under the homogenized name of Presidents' Day. Move over George and Abe, and come right in Millard Fillmore and William Henry Harrison . . . not to mention some of the more recent dandies.

Not everyone is totally impressed with the need for a day of rest honoring our presidents. A young mother of two elementary pupils—she will remain unidentified because so few share her feelings—put it this way:

"Instead of giving my children a day out of school, which most likely will be spent in front of the TV or in a mall, why aren't they in school and perhaps spending the entire day learning more about George Washington, Abraham Lincoln and all of the other presidents?"

She has a point, you know. And it's even more valid for those of us who live in a part of the country where school is out every time there is snow or even a forecast of snow.

The same could be said for Martin Luther King Day. Instead of closing school and turning children loose to do who knows what, why don't we keep them in school and spend the day learning about Martin Luther King, Frederick Douglass, George Washington Carver and others who have contributed so much.

But we don't do things like that, do we?

Instead, we honor two of our greatest presidents—and others not so great—with a holiday known for big sales and a paid holiday for all government workers while local, state and national budgets are so far out of whack they will never be corrected.

It's enough to make George and Abe turn over in their graves. Repeatedly.

February, 1995

A write-in vote for a special stamp

Memo: To the Citizens' Stamp Advisory Committee (whoever you are and wherever you hang out when you advise the U.S. Postal Service what to put on our postage stamps):

I suppose you folks are pretty excited about the Elvis Presley stamp coming out this week. You should be. It's been a public relations bonanza for post offices everywhere.

Post offices don't get a whole lot of favorable publicity. Usually, people are complaining about the price of stamps going up, long lines, no place to park. You know what I'm saying?

But then you came up with the idea to put Elvis on a stamp and wow! You have been getting all kinds of good PR.

That idea of letting folks vote on which picture of Elvis to put on the stamp was a dandy. Did one of your committee people think of that or did a high-power Madison Avenue agency earn big bucks by coming up with that idea?

Regardless, it really got the public involved in casting ballots that decided to use the young, handsome Elvis instead of the old, tired, bloated-looking Elvis. Good choice.

There more than likely will be a stampede when the first stamps go on sale at 12:01 a.m. Friday—the 58th anniversary of his birth—at the Graceland Post Office down in Memphis. I suspect that all of the souvenir shops will be open late (or early) so that Uncle Sam's Postal Service won't be the only one making money that night.

I doubt that I'll be able to drive down to Graceland to buy my stamps of the King. I'll just wait until daylight and get mine here at home. I heard (maybe I better change that to read) that they won't go on sale at the post offices until noon Friday. Wonder why that is?

Do you think I might be able to find a postal clerk who will bootleg me a few as soon as the post office opens or sometime during the morning? I wouldn't try to resell them for a profit or anything like that. I just want to try to beat those long lines and maybe find a parking place before the crowd arrives.

I also heard (doggonit, make that read; I can't say heard when I'm writing for a newspaper) that the post office is going to print 300 million Elvis stamps, about twice as many as usual for a commemorative stamp. That caused one fellow I know to say there's been so many reports Elvis is still alive that a lot of folks probably will buy stamps because they figure if you can't join him, lick him.

I didn't say that; I just hear . . . read it.

I also understand that the Elvis stamp is going to be just the first of a series called "Legends of American Music."

There are supposed to be rock 'n' roll and rhythm and blues stamps of Bill Haley, Buddy Holly, Clyde McPhatter, Richie Valens, Otis Redding and Dinah Washington, in addition to Elvis.

If you like Broadway musicals, you'll find stamps for Oklahoma!, My Fair Lady, and Porgy and Bess early this year.

What I'm really waiting for is the country & western series with Hank Williams, the Carter Family, Patsy Cline and Bob Wills. They're not due out until September, so I might get some of them on my birthday cards.

I was kind of hoping for a Billy Ray Cyrus, but I guess you have to be dead 10 years before you can get on a stamp. I can wait if Billy Ray can.

Well, Committee, that brings me to a request I'd like to make.

I know you put out all kinds of stamps for special occasions. We received Christmas cards with all kinds of pretty designs. There were three or four different stamps showing the American flag. A couple saluted Kentucky's bicentennial, some had that wood duck on them and one had a white bengal tiger.

I also know of at least eight stamps that say love on them.

What I want, though, is a stamp to put on letters when I'm paying bills. I certainly don't want to put a love stamp on an envelope when I'm paying the cable or sewer bill. No way! I'll use 29 of those one-centers many people leave hanging in the stamp machines before I'll lick a love stamp to pay a bill.

What I'd really like to use is something like a big, old python squeezing the last penny out of our household budget. Or perhaps that white tiger ready to pounce. Or maybe an attack wood duck.

Anything but a love message. 'Preciate anything you can do.

January, 1993

Counting noses, asking questions

250,000,001, 250,000,002, 250,000,003, 250,00 . . .

Hold it just a cotton-pickin' minute! Who's the wise guy who moved out there western Kentucky?

How do you expect us to get this dad-blasted census done right if you all don't stand still just for a few minutes?

Now we have to start all over!

250,000,001, 250,000,002 . . .

OK, so that's not exactly the way they're doing this every-10-year nose count. But it should work. It worked for many of us when we were in the service and some gravel-voiced sergeant would order us to count off. And in gym class, when we'd count off and then the teacher would put all the evens on one team and the odds on another.

Some high guy (or gal) in the government could pick out a certain day and time for us all to fall out and count off. A Sunday would be the best day. Sundays seem to work best for elections in Europe. They always have far better turnouts of voters than we do on Tuesdays.

Coming up with a best time would be another matter. We have to work it in after church but before the stores open. There would have been no problem a few years ago when the old Sunday blue laws prohibited business on the Sabbath.

We can work out something. And as long as we get finished before April 9, we won't have to worry about anybody driving to Cincinnati for a baseball game.

A count like this surely would be a lot cheaper than the way the Bureau of the Census is going to do it.

The cost of the 1990 census—the 21st time since it was decided we should keep track of how many of us there are—has been estimated in print and by the talking heads from as little as $1.4 billion to as much as $2.6 billion.

Hah! That lower figure surely was a typographical error. We know that our government isn't going to do anything for $1.4 billion when it can do the same thing for $2.6 billion. Government doesn't work that way. Never has, never will. And the census is government.

So $2.6 billion it is.

Estimates have pegged the 1990 census at 250,000,000. A

28

little grade school long division, 250,000,000 into 2,600,000,000, cancel six zeroes on each side . . . Forget that. Get a calculator. It figures out to $10.40 to count each one of us.

Wow! That's expensive. Maybe we should change the census to every 15 years, just to hold the cost down. We can't do that, though, because the Constitution says every 10 years. So be it.

Do you suppose the Census Bureau could just send us the $20.40 it will cost to count the people at our house? We can just count ourselves and tell the people in Washington to add 2 to whatever figure they come up with.

That probably wouldn't work, however, because the Census Bureau wants to know other stuff, too. Such as name, sex, racial or ethnic group, age, marital status, how all household members are related. Do we own our house or rent? Nosy-type questions.

And that's only if the questionnaire we should have received March 23 is the short form—only 14 questions.

About one in six households will receive the long form, which not only asks the 14 questions on the short form but 44 more as well. The long form wants to know more about your housing, citizenship, education, work hours and location, how you get there. It even wants to know if perhaps you commute by ferryboat.

You're supposed to return the questionnaire by April 1. The Census Bureau figures 80 percent of us will. Census workers will start calling on the other 20 percent after April 30 to fill in the cracks.

The final tally is supposed to be on President Bush's desk by Dec. 31. Not too long after the first of the year, each state will begin receiving the statistics necessary to redraw legislative districts, figure out how to distribute various federal and state funds and hundreds of other official things.

But the 1990 census will be outdated even before it's finished. Thousands counted by April 1 will be dead by April 2. And thousands upon thousands more will be born between the time the counting is finished and the day Bush gets the final, official count.

If we could just get everyone to fall out Sunday and count off. It would probably be just as accurate, maybe moreso. And a heck of a lot cheaper.

March, 1990

Spare the rod . . . you know the rest

A half century ago, there was a rule at our house, for boys and girls alike: If any of us got a paddling at school, we could expect to get another one when we got home that evening.

It was a rule in effect in most homes in that era, and more

than a few out of that generation will have you know the busting they got at home was far worse than the one laid on them by a teacher or the principal.

That rule was a deterrent of sorts against acting up in school. When it came to paddlings, two for the price of one was no bargain at all.

Of course, as we got older we wised up a little and figured out that our parents really didn't have to know if a teacher had introduced us to the board of education that day. But more often than not, the word got home some way, particularly if you had younger brothers and sisters at the same school. Then you really got it. First for acting up, then for not 'fessing up.

Nowadays, paddling is perhaps the most controversial issue in education. Nineteen states have banned corporal punishment, two words which in themselves sound so much more severe than a paddling.

In some states, local or county districts may set their own policies.

USA TODAY newspaper reported recently that "This year, for the first time in history, more than half of our students—52%—will be going to school where corporal punishment has been banned."

Perhaps that is good. And perhaps it is not.

There are strong arguments for either position. Opponents of paddling relate stories of vicious beatings, and they do happen, make no mistake about it. But such cases are rare, very rare, and there are ways of dealing with teachers who are guilty of this type of abuse.

But most paddlings any of us ever got in school—and the ones our children and grandchildren get today—are three or four swats on the butt that hurt our pride far more than our backside.

Take away the threat of the paddle and what tools of discipline are left for our teachers? And whether we want to admit it or not, and very few of us will, the discipline many children get at school is the only discipline they ever get.

Extra homework, loss of privileges aren't the answer. What do you do when the punished pupil doesn't do his extra homework? Pile on more, which won't be done either?

When was the last time you read or heard anything good about schools? They're the most criticized, most maligned institutions in existence. Some people don't pull any punches and say our schools are among the worst in the world.

Not all of us share that opinion. Some of us see it as a copout by others who aren't doing their share and are looking for the most logical scapegoat.

All of us had some very good teachers when we were in school, but with one or two exceptions, they weren't as good as our children's teachers and their children's teachers.

Today's teachers are better trained and face stiffer requirements for certification. In Kentucky, teachers must obtain a master's degree within 10 years of their bachelor's or out they go.

Yet we put these teachers in classrooms, tell them the only discipline they can employ is a frown and a threat to take away privileges and reduce them to highly educated baby-sitters.

What a shame! What a waste of talented and dedicated people who could and would make our schools the best in the world if their hands weren't tied by silly, unneeded laws passed by people who haven't been in a classroom for years.

There was a teacher at a little high school here in Southern Ohio who really lowered the boom on me in the spring of 1946. Sometimes I think I can still feel it. I may have lost a little dignity—another complaint by the anti-paddling people—but I learned who was boss in that classroom. I deserved what I got (although I made sure my Dad never found out about it) and to this day I consider that teacher among the best four or five I ever had.

Spare the rod and spoil the child, the saying goes. Or at least it used to. It may be too late to revive that adage. Too many of today's children already are spoiled and the best teachers of the world can't do anything about it.

September, 1989

Debates? Comic has better idea

About those so-called debates:

Was it really necessary to have four? Was it even necessary to have three? Two? Or even one?

Have we made any progress toward an informed electorate? Is there even any such thing as an informed electorate?

If there is, it didn't become that way because of anything presented in the first two so-called debates. It took a much stronger stomach than mine to tune in Thursday night for Round 3 in Richmond, Va., and only true gluttons for punishment will come back Monday night for the grand finale in East Lansing, Mich.

It's nights such as those that make you thankful—but not overly—for cable.

OK, now that all the Republicans are upset with me on one hand and all the Democrats are heating tar and plucking chickens on the other, answer me this:

Unless you've been out of the country and/or haven't seen a newspaper or listened to TV and radio for the last four years or more, what did you hear or see on the debates that you didn't already know?

Nothing. Zilch. Zero.

Well, maybe you did hear a couple of things that were enlightening.

You heard poor old Jim Stockdale, Ross Perot's running-mate-by-default, define himself aptly—"Who am I? Why am I here?"—and do an even better job of defining Washington and everyone in it, "And I think America is seeing right now the reason this nation is in gridlock."

So who's winning the debates? Ask a Clinton supporter and there's no question about it: Clinton and Gore. Ask a Bush backer and he's equally confident: Bush and Quayle.

These people had their minds made up as far back as the party conventions. Nothing has changed their minds and nothing is going to.

Who's the loser? Sad to say, perhaps all of us.

Hey, we really don't have a whole heck of a lot to choose from.

We have a sitting president who asked us to "Read my lips . . ." and, except for the unpleasantness in the Middle East, hasn't done a whole lot since.

We have a governor from a state that ranks 48th, 49th, 50th in just about everything there is to be ranked but he's going to lead us to the promised land.

We read George's lips, he still raised taxes; Willie's slicker than snake oil.

And, of course, there's Mr. Perot. First, he was going to run. Then he wasn't. Now he's running again. He still has a little more than two weeks in which to change his mind again. And again. In this election year in which Larry King, Arsenio Hall, Phil Donahue—did anyone visit Oprah and Sally?—have emerged as the leading public opinion shapers, here's a plug for another one, perhaps the wisest of them all.

Remember Jimmy Walker, the long-necked, loud-mouthed black man who played J.J.—or maybe it was Jay-Jay, whatever—on the sitcom "Good Times" what seems like centuries ago?

He was on someone's show a couple of weeks ago at about a quarter till one in the morning. He bemoaned having to choose between Bush and Clinton—Perot was on the sideline at the time—and suggested "we go to all the candidates for president and tell them to forget it, we're not going to elect a president this year."

Walker suggested we simply go without one for the next four years. Why not? We couldn't get in much worse shape than we're in now.

His idea might fly with one amendment: Give Congress its walking papers, too.

October, 1992

32

If this is a joke, no one's laughing

Hello, Daily Times? I'd like to talk to someone concerning the story in the paper the other day about the 131 prisoners out at Lucasville asking for damages they say they suffered in the prison riot last April.

That was just a joke, wasn't it? I mean they don't really think the state should pay them for trouble they started, do they? It must be a joke, that's for sure.

Can you imagine the state shelling out $825,000 for inmates' property losses and injuries they're blaming on a riot they started? Hey, that's really funny.

Who's going to pay for the millions of dollars in damage they caused to the cells in L Block? I suppose all that was caused by the five guards who were held hostage for 11 days. They probably were just tearing the place to pieces and all those prisoners couldn't stop them.

And who's going to pay for all the overtime by prison personnel and the State Patrol, plus all the expense of calling out the National Guard?

Hey, maybe the state could make a deal with them. The state can agree to pay $825,000 to those prisoners and then all 400 who were in L Block could pay the state the millions and millions of dollars it's going to take to get the penitentiary back the way it was last Easter. And, of course, the inmates could also pick up the tab for everyone on duty out there for those 11 days.

They probably wouldn't go for that, would they? I doubt it.

You know the one that really kills me . . . sorry, poor choice of words. Let me put it another way: You know the one that really irritates (That's much, much better, isn't it?) me? It's that one guy who wants the state to pay him $740,000 for his seven years of legal research!

That figures out to better than $105,000 a year for his jailhouse work. I bet a lot of lawyers in town would trade their 1992 earnings for what that con's wanting.

I wonder what in the world that guy was researching. Sounds to me as if someone out at Lucasville had an awful lot of free time on his hands during the last seven years. Don't those guys have any work to do? Put them to work restoring L Block; that ought to keep them busy for a while.

And another thing: What kind of resources do they have out there that would let a guy do research he figures is worth more than those guards would earn in 25 or 30 years? That must be a dandy law library.

The most scary part of all this is that some judge will probably award him a good bit of what he's asking for.

The next most scary part is who is going to pay it in the

long run: we taxpayers. However much of that $825,000 is paid to inmates for riot losses might have been used to help improve our schools and colleges. Or it could have helped build a highway or repair a bridge.

But what can you expect when we spend more every year to keep a prisoner out at Lucasville than we do to educate our children! Crazy old world, isn't it?

Now I can sympathize—but not much—with those guys wanting to be reimbursed for their toothbrushes, food and pictures. But jewelry, TV sets and stereos? No way! Absolutely, no way! Do you mean to tell me they have their own TV's and stereos in their cells? Why can't they watch and listen in their recreation rooms the way we did when we were in the Army? I can't believe this.

Another thing I can't believe is those prisoners asking damages for mental stress.

If they want to talk about mental stress, let them talk to the hostages and their families or the families of the nine prisoners they killed. Let them talk to the family of the guard whom they killed. Let them talk to just about anyone who lives in Lucasville. Those people can tell those prisoners a thing or two about stress.

That story would have been a good one to have saved and run in the paper next April Fools' Day. It's really funny.

What? You say it's no joke? It's really for real?

I kind of thought so. I don't hear anyone laughing.

August, 1993

One of the Michaels on a big-bucks bill?

In case you missed it, there is big news in the world of money.

Wait a minute, wait a minute . . . don't get so excited. You (and I) aren't going to get a lot of it—unless we hit the lottery, rob a bank, inherit a bundle from a wealthy uncle or some other such thing happens. Life doesn't work that way very often, does it?

What is going to happen is that Uncle Sam's printers are going to give our paper money a new look.

Can't you just see it now! Reach into your billfold and pull out a $100 bill and it may have the portrait of Michael Jackson on it. Who knows whose picture is on a big one now? I haven't seen a hundred-dollar bill since the Army paymaster counted out my mustering-out pay in '53.

A $50 bill, which I think now carries the likeness of Ulysses Grant, could be updated with Michael Jordan, Kirby Puckett, Jose Conseco, Shaq or even David Letterman. Why not? Athletes

34

and entertainers have all the money anyway, don't they? The last common man I recall with a big bundle was Sam Walton and he's not with us anymore.

There might be a problem finding pictures to put on $20, $10, $5, $2 and $1 denominations. Ball players, movie idols, rock stars and others like them would be insulted to be pictured on something so comparatively worthless.

What a pity. Some of them would be great candidates if the government ever decided to print a $3 bill.

But let's back up a minute. I got it all wrong. They're not going to change any of the pictures. What they're going to do is make the portraits a little larger. It's one of several changes being considered to make it more difficult for counterfeiters.

The bogus bill boys are getting so good—the result of new technology and a lot of practice—that $166 million in phony bills were seized last year, according to the Secret Service, which keeps track of such things in addition to jogging with Bill and protecting Hillary, Al and Tipper.

They're just going to enlarge the portraits, not the bills themselves. That's a relief! If they ever decided to increase the size of bills to keep up with the rate of inflation, we could paper the living room walls with a few ones and still get back some change.

The Treasury said it plans to have some new designs ready sometime next year and will begin circulating new bills about a year later. Thank goodness for the early warning; some of the changes could cause problems.

For instance, one of the ideas to foil funny-money crooks is what is described as color-shifting ink. You look at a bill straight on and it is green, which is what greenbacks are supposed to look like. But viewed from an angle, it will appear to be gold. That could be very, very confusing.

Ditto for another idea: computer-designed interactive patterns. Didn't you just know computers would be involved some way? Well, let me tell you, Mr. Moneymaker, and I speak with the voice of experience. You hit the wrong key on your computer, as many of us do frequently, and the entire U.S. Mint's production for that day will disappear into thin air. Rich air, but thin.

What these interactive patterns are supposed to do is turn wavy when illegally copied. Picture some poor soul sitting in a bar after a drink or two. Everything looks wavy. He's sitting there clutching a fistful of counterfeit money and thinks it looks wavy because he's had one too many Jack Daniel's.

The Treasury also is thinking about putting iridescent planchettes in the paper it prints money on. Does that sound like something you want in your billfold or money clip? It could be contagious, for all we know.

Most of us probably couldn't care less about what our money looks like. Instead of redesigning, we would be much more interested in some kind of redistribution.

However, it has been 65 years since any changes have been made in how our money looks. All of it, except the short-lived Susan B. Anthony dollar coin, commemorates white males with odd hair styles and funny-looking clothes. The politically correct crowd pounces on nearly everything written or said dealing with race or gender. Yet it lets the Treasury get away with racism, sexism and bad-hairism.

It's time for change . . . and I don't mean a handful of coins.

August, 1994

Does anyone know what time it is?

If you correctly followed the one simple instruction everyone must heed the last Sunday in October—spring forward, fall back—you arrived at church at the proper time this morning.

You slipped into your pew just as the choir was getting ready with its first anthem and the smiling preacher was preparing to give you his blessing.

If you forgot, you and a few equally forgetful friends no doubt wondered where everyone else was. You were an hour early, which explains why you found a parking place so close to the church.

And if you really pulled a boo-boo and turned the little hand in the wrong direction, you got there just as the rest of the congregation was coming out the front door and starting for home.

Silly, isn't it? Blame it on the Uniform Time Act, passed by Congress in 1967. That law requires us to tinker with our timepieces in the spring, running them ahead an hour in observance of Daylight Saving Time.

Six months later—today—we apparently have saved enough daylight to get us through the winter, so we're advised to fall back. We reset all of our clocks and watches—and don't forget those @$#&%*! blinking VCR's—and that takes off Daylight Saving Time and restores Eastern Standard Time.

Which means when we get to work and school tomorrow, all of the clocks will be wrong and people will be running around in circles of confusion while trying to remember what they're supposed to do.

It doesn't have to be like this.

In the beginning, when God said, "Let there be light," He simply "called the light Day and the darkness He called Night."

He didn't say one word about Standard Time or Daylight Saving Time or any other kind of time. His system worked pretty well for centuries.

But then Congress looked around for something it hadn't already screwed up and someone's eyes came to rest on a clock. That did it. Times haven't been the same since.

When is the last time you asked a friend for the time and he looked at a sundial? No use; sundials can't be adjusted for Daylight Saving Time. They're pretty and nice to have sitting out on the lawn or patio. But worthless if you really are concerned about the correct time.

Come to think of it, how do we know the time is correct anytime?

The Uniform Time Act divided the United States and its possessions into eight Standard Time zones. Most of us are acquainted with the big four—Eastern, Central, Mountain and Pacific. That's how we know to turn on the TV at 5 p.m. so we can see the Big 10 (11??) lose the Rose Bowl in a game that starts three hours earlier according to California clocks.

But there are four more: Atlantic, Yukon, Alaska-Hawaii and Bering (Samoa). Where are they? Who knows? And how do we know what they're doing with all of their Daylight Saved Time.

Actually, as we all know, we don't really save any daylight. We simply move it from the start of the day to the end. In the fall, vice versa.

Some like it, some don't. As a rule, daylight time is more popular in urban areas because it gives more time for outdoor activities. Rural folk aren't particularly happy because they lose morning light and because no one remembers to tell the livestock to adjust their clocks.

Fewer auto accidents and traffic fatalities are credited to Daylight Saving Time by the U.S. Department of Transportation, which oversees the time law.

Wait a minute. The Department of Transportation? What does it have to do with clocks and time? How come time isn't the responsibility of the Labor or Agriculture departments? Or Energy? Even the Treasury might be more appropriate, inasmuch as saving is involved.

That sounds like something Congress would do. It probably doesn't even know what time it is. Does anyone really know?

October, 1990

He's sociable, and very secure

"When'd you get that answering contraption on your phone?" were the first words I heard. They were followed quickly by, "You too busy to talk to your friends anymore?"

Oh, Lord, I sighed. What did I do to deserve this? I wasn't

serious, of course, because the caller was one of my oldest friends, going all the way back to grade-school days. I won't tell you his name or where he lives for two reasons: 1. I didn't ask his permission, and 2. There may be some outstanding warrants for him.

The answering machine has been in place for a little more than a year now and we still try to answer our phone every time it rings. If we're at home, that is, and I'm not taking a nap and have the ringer turned off.

I don't like answering machines anymore than you do, I assured him. But it was a gift from one of our kids and you never know when your children might call, don't get an answer and wonder why Mom and Dad aren't using the answering machine we got them. It will remain hooked up as long as it works properly, and sometimes we have serious doubts whether it does all the time.

But you didn't call to talk about my answering machine. It's been at least a year and a half since you last called. Something must be bugging you and I know you're dying to tell.

He snickered, then resumed control of the conversation.

"Well, I was just wondering why none of you newspaper people hadn't had anything to say about those Social Security big shots getting all those big-buck bonuses for the fine job they're doing up there in Washington," he explained.

"And this is only a few weeks after I read where Social Security is going to run out of money in 20 or 25 years. They're talking about cutting next year's cost-of-living raise and taking more out of workers' paychecks and maybe even raising the age when you can retire and start drawing it."

Well, I guess I did read something about the Social Security Administration giving its employees some bonuses, I replied, but . . .

"But hell," he interrupted. "They didn't just give out SOME bonuses, they passed out $32 billion worth! And they gave one guy, who already makes more than $120,000 a year, a bonus of $9,256! And he had been working there less than three months!"

I didn't need an answering machine now. I didn't even need a phone. His voice had become so loud that I'm sure I could have heard him from the next county without one.

"That fellow with his big salary got a bonus that is more than a lot of people on Social Security receive in an entire year. Don't you understand what I'm trying to say?"

There must have been a reason for $32 million in bonuses, I managed to squeeze in, but that does seem like a lot of money. And I have to admit, I don't expect ever to get a $9,000-plus bonus.

"I thought some of you people might write something about this," my friend said, his voice much calmer now. "But the only one I've heard raising any Cain is that congressman from Northern Kentucky, Jim Bunning. You know who I mean, the old baseball pitcher. He's throwing some high hard ones at Social Security."

Jim's a good man . . . , I attempted to say.

"Hey, you're on Social Security now, aren't you?" he served up a high hard one of his own.

You know good and well I am, I told him. You know I had to retire on Social Security Disability a few years ago and . . .

"Well that beats all," he interrupted. "You're afraid to write anything about Social Security, ain't you? You're afraid one of those guys in Washington will review your case and cut you off."

"Doggone! I never would have thought it. I bet you'll never write anything about the IRS, either. Or police speed traps, unsolved murders, plea bargaining, basketball referees or your barber.

"You're afraid one of them will get even. I bet you won't write anything about your mother-in-law, either!"

May, 1994

3-Me 'n' Norm

Her first name really is

Norma. But for some reason, most

likely laziness on my part,

she has answered to the

abbreviated version since the

day we met. We now have

45 years worth of unused a-a-a-a-'s

and no idea of what we'll ever

do with them.

She would rather be lucky than good

My wife is one of the luckiest women on earth.

Not because she's my wife—good heavens, no! She deserves a medal or something for that. She's lucky because good things just seem to happen for her.

Example: She can spot a coin on the sidewalk, in the parking lot or on the street when we're walking from half a block away. Even tell if it's heads or tails. How would you like to have a woman with an eye like that watching you for 40 years?

Her luck got a real test about a week ago.

It happened something like this:

We got home about 7 p.m. It had been a long but very pleasant day, starting with a trip to nearby Ironton for a covered-dish luncheon and speaking engagement for the DMA (Don't Mention Age) Fellowship of Calvary Baptist Church.

Next stop was Huntington Mall across the river in West Virginia to exchange a Christmas gift that didn't fit. That's another bit of convincing proof that people should shop at home. If the undersized gift had been bought in the town where we live, an hour-long trip and all the resulting confusion and consternation wouldn't have happened.

But that's another story.

Anyway, after several hours of loafing, very little buying and failure to find the correct size in the blankety-blank Christmas gift, we returned home.

"I've lost my mother's ring!" wailed my wife, who at that moment didn't feel a bit lucky at all. When she said mother's ring, she didn't mean a ring belonging to her mother. She meant mother's ring as in symbolic of membership in that worldwide sisterhood whose members have paid their dues through years of changing diapers, wiping noses, sitting up nights with youngsters down with croup, measles or any one of thousands of childhood illnesses and, finally, more long nights of first dates, first car dates, proms and other social events that turn mothers gray and unsociable. She just knew she had lost it.

"I took it and my wedding rings off to put lotion on my hands," she recalled. "I must have laid it in my lap and when I got out of the car, it fell into the street. If I'd been wearing slacks instead of a skirt, it would still have been in the car."

Women understand that kind of logic; men don't try.

Personally, I'm just glad she remembered to put the other rings back on. The mother's ring didn't cost all that much, just three little birthstones on a gold band that was purchased about 25 years ago when it was decided once and for all that there wouldn't be a fourth.

But we had to look for it.

Early the next morning we were back in Ironton, about 20

miles away, searching along the sidewalk where we had parked just a few doors down from Calvary Baptist Church. We raked through the frosty leaves, pop bottle caps and dog-doo. But there wasn't a ring to be found.

Surely she didn't expect to drive on to Huntington to search that mammoth mall parking lot? Surely, she did.

Not a word was said until we pulled into the parking lot, trying to figure which acre we had parked in about 12 hours before.

I think we were about where that pickup truck is pulling in now, I suggested. We headed in that direction as the young woman driving maneuvered the truck into the space.

"We're going to look under your truck," said my spouse, who on this day was wearing a simple wedding band, much like those found in Crackerjack boxes. "We were here yesterday and I lost my ring—"

"Well, there it is!" said the younger of the two women in the truck. She was pointing to a spot about a foot from where my most lucky wife stood.

I'm trying to persuade her to buy some lottery tickets. Or go to a bingo game. Maybe even to a racetrack. We really should.

January, 1991

The best umbrellas are the ones that are lost

Umbrellas are overrated.

They're supposed to keep you dry. They seldom do, unless it's a beautiful day and you're using one for a sun screen.

But let the skies open up and the rain pour down and you're better off leaving the umbrella wherever you normally forget it and making a run for it. You'll stay almost as dry and won't run into anything.

We have several umbrellas at our house. All but one are lost. That one just happened to be in the back seat of the car a few days ago when the predicted partly cloudy started falling in big drops.

It is impossible to sit in the driver's side of the car, stick an umbrella out the door, raise it and get under it without getting the front part of your body soaked.

Never mind that your back is still dry. Its turn will come when you return to the car. Then, you not only have to hold the umbrella outside while you back into the seat, you also have to close it and complete one of three maneuvers:

1. Push it across to the passenger seat, wiping hundreds of clinging raindrops into your lap.

2. Wrap it around your neck while trying to deposit it in the back seat, while carefully avoiding all the pointy parts trying to

42

poke you in the eyes.

3. Stand bravely in the rain while you close the @#*$&! thing, confident that you can't get any wetter than you already are.

Umbrellas don't do the job they are supposed to do. It's obvious they were designed by a committee.

One of the best moves in recent years was made when umbrellas were banned from a great many football stadiums. Countless eyes were saved. Besides, the only people who ever saw a single play of a rainy-day game were those in the very first row.

Their umbrellas blocked the view of the people in the row behind them, the second row of umbrellas shut out the people in the third row and on and on until the people in the top row of bleachers could see nothing but the top row of umbrellas across the field.

And that was the good part.

The bad part is that all of the runoff from front-row umbrellas is deposited directly into the lap of second-row spectators and the second-row rain goes . . . well, you know the rest.

This deep-rooted animosity against umbrellas, particularly at sporting events, goes back to the late 1960s. The University of Cincinnati and Ohio University hooked up in a point-a-minute shootout in a cold, wind-blown downpour.

The woman I take to football games insisted she must have some hot chocolate. I normally refuse to go to the concession stand while the game is going on, but it didn't look as if anything could happen. After all, there was less than a minute left in the half and OU was nearly 80 yards away from the UC goal.

This game was being played in UC's old stadium, which had a top deck added to handle Cincinnati Bengals games before a new and larger stadium was built. UC always had small crowds, and the weather made certain this would no exception. There was no one seated within miles of us.

Returning from the trek to the concession stand on another level, I glanced at the scoreboard. It had changed. OU had scored.

What happened? I asked.

"Nothing," was the shivering reply.

What do you mean "nothing"? OU has more points. What happened?

"I don't know, Jim," she wailed. "They just got in a big pile and the referee threw his hands up in the air and signaled touchdown."

The rest of the story came out after the game when we met some friends who had spent the afternoon in a warm, dry press

43

box across the field. We started talking about what we had seen.

"But the highlight of the game," declared one of the dry friends, "was that crazy lady chasing her umbrella all over the upper deck. She'd catch up with it and bend down to pick it up and here'd come another gust of wind and off they'd go . . ."

She never took another umbrella to a football game, I guarantee it.

September, 1991

This bath is for the birds

"What we need now," said the woman who decides what we need around our house, "is a bird bath."

What we really need, I thought to myself, failing to hear her last four words, is to hit the Ohio lottery. Or maybe the Kentucky lottery. Or any lottery with a lot of dollars. That's the only answer.

We don't have any wealthy relatives who are about to check out. We don't have any wealthy relatives period. Our relatives are healthy instead of wealthy.

Signing a professional sports contract is out, too, but just barely. Only two things stand in the way: too much age and not enough talent.

A rock star perhaps? Not a chance. I don't even know the first verse of "Achy Breaky Heart." Come to think of it, I don't know the first line.

Wait a minute! There's one sure-fire way to get rich: Get elected to Congress.

But before I could even take out petitions, those last four words of the first paragraph soaked in.

Bird bath? Did you really say bird bath? What in the @#$*&+%! do we need with a bird bath?

"I think a bird bath would be nice," you-know-who replied calmly. Almost sweetly. Very aggravatingly. "Besides, we've lived here more than three years now and you still haven't put up our bird feeder."

What's that got to do with it? If they can't be fat, you want them to be clean, huh?

"That isn't even funny," she fired back, and without hesitation: "I think a bird bath would be fun. You know there are so many different kinds of birds out there. I'd enjoy sitting on the back porch with my binoculars and bird book and learning the different kinds of birds."

Big deal. There are only four kinds: big ones, little ones, pretty ones and ugly ones. Lots of ugly ones, those big old fat black ones. What do you call them, grackles?

"I don't know," Miss Eveready Answer responded. "But buy

44

me a bird bath and I'll get my binoculars and bird book and tell you."

Geeeez! What do we need with a bird bath? They keep themselves clean now, don't they? I haven't seen nor heard of any dirty birds since George Gobel died.

No response. Just a withering look.

OK, say that we do get a bird bath. The next thing you know we'll need separate his and hers baths, properly identified.

If we go the unisex route, there'll be trouble for certain the first time some creeper warbles a few fowl notes to the wrong little chickadee. All because you wanted a bird bath.

And that's just the beginning.

We buy a bird bath and the next thing you'll be looking for will be a sale on teensy, tiny bath towels. And bathrobes.

You'll never find enough pairs of little flip-flops for them to put on their funny little feet when they finish their baths. And I'm certainly not going to climb any trees to gather up the soiled towels. No way will I install a flock of little feather dryers.

It doesn't pay to be a smart aleck. We bought a bird bath, just as I knew we would do all along.

We don't need any little towels, robes, flip-flops or dryers.

What we do need is about a half dozen tiny portapotties. His and hers, of course.

July, 1992

More than one way to get burned at beach

The first time the people at our house went to the beach was in 1969.

Before that, none of us had ever before seen a beach. We didn't even have a clue to how much fun the combination of water, sand and sun could be.

The closest we had ever come to a beach was the banks of the Ohio River. A lot of what we had thought was sand was really mud. The shores across the river in Kentucky looked like real sand, but there was no way to get there.

And Lakes Jackson and Vesuvius! Now there were real beaches. But, as a kid, they were so far away. I was lucky to get there more than a couple of times a year; a school picnic, perhaps, and maybe a family reunion where you had to put up with show-off relatives who could dive and swim and do all the other things 97-pound weaklings could only dream of.

So that first trip to Myrtle Beach was more than a treat. It was the thrill of a lifetime.

It was also suntan lotion, followed a few hours later by twice as much calamine lotion in usually futile attempts to ease the pain of a world-class sunburn.

For 24 years since that first trip, we have gone at least once and often twice to a Carolina, Florida or Alabama beach for a few days of fun (?) in the sun. And for exactly the same number of years, the woman I rub lotion on has suffered a sunburn. Big time.

It's not that I don't do the lotion thing properly; I do a great job and enjoy every second of it. But she doesn't know when enough is enough.

"I'm not even pink yet," she'll say. "Just let me stay out here another half hour."

Another half hour is usually at least 45 minutes too long. What wasn't even pink yet in reality is scarlet. In a day or two, she looks like a glazed doughnut from the day-old counter. And then the peeling starts. Ughhh!

It happened again on our last visit to Florida. I shouldn't have been surprised. But this was the third week in October, for heaven's sake! The woman simply has no sense of time.

The almost-winter sunburn was the second most shocking event of our trip.

The first was the signs at a shop in Panama City. One, in very large letters, advertised "Machine-gun Lessons." The other made it known that the rapid-fire weapons were available for rent.

Understand, please, that these signs weren't in the war zone of Miami and surrounding south Florida. They were miles and miles away in the Panhandle where normal people live.

Excuse me. I'm just a dumb country boy. Is it normal to use your lunch hour or stop in after work for machine-gun lessons? Is renting a machine-gun like stopping in at the video store and picking up a movie?

"Did you get a movie, Dad? What are we going to watch tonight?"

"No, son, I didn't rent a movie. But wait till you see what I did get. It's a machine-gun. Hurry and eat your supper and we'll go out and fire a few rounds. But remember, we have to clean it before we take it back in the morning."

Lord, help us.

November, 1993

There's always something cooking at our house

"When we get this house back in order," the woman I share this disorderly house with commented the other day, "I want you to start getting back into the kitchen and doing some cooking."

Well, where else would I cook? I thought to myself, because those kinds of thoughts are better kept to oneself or voiced only in an otherwise empty room. The guest bedroom, perhaps?

Certainly not in my den! There will be no sauteing, parboiling or any of that culinary stuff there, you can bet your last spatula on that.

Disorderly house? Hey, I didn't mean THAT kind of disorderly house. I'm talking disorderly as in cluttered. Topsy turvy. All messed up. Two rooms of furniture stacked in one for painting and wallpapering. Then vice versa. No curtains at the windows. That kind of disorderly.

That's a way of life at our house. It's been like that for 39 years, 11 1/2 months. My wife changes paint, paper, curtains etc. more often than I change underwear.

OK, that is a slight exaggeration. I don't really change underwear that often.

When we moved to our current home one year and 49 weeks ago, we agreed it was just what we were looking for. Perfect. We could move right in and not have to do a thing.

Anyone who believes that . . .

You know those orange and white cones and barrels that you usually find about 50 yards before a sign that proclaims "Your tax dollars at work"? That's what our perfect house that was just what we were looking for has resembled for the better part of two years.

I'm not real crazy about that living room carpet, my interior decorator mumbled even before we bought the house. That was a strong hint of things to come.

That living room carpet has got to go, she said in her best construction foreman voice only a day or two later.

Since then, the wallpaper and paint in the bathrooms and the master bedroom have met the same fate. An oversized hall on the second level was remodeled and became a normal-sized hall and really nice laundry room.

Now she was really getting warmed up.

In the last two months there have been such commands as I want a wall here, a partition there, take that planter out, extend this wall two feet. You can't do that or you don't want to do that, relatives and friends cautioned. But she and the man we hired to do all of those things did.

This was a six-room house with an oversized upstairs hall when we bought it. It now has seven rooms, plus a laundry room. About the only thing that remains the same is that it's a split level. She hasn't figured out how to get everything on one floor. Yet.

So I'm not overly concerned about getting back into the kitchen and doing some cooking for a while yet. It could be weeks. Or months. Or even this time next year.

But I can cook.

In fact, I used to do quite a bit of it during the BC days. That's Before Cholesterol. A lot of my favorite recipes were

47

retired when we learned what all of that cheese and eggs could do to arteries.

I don't mean to brag—to be honest, I really do—but a couple of my recipes are about to be published in a school cookbook in Northern Kentucky. One is a breakfast casserole for which the key ingredients are calories and cholesterol. The other is a yummy cherry streusel.

I used to have a lot more, but for some reason they were always being misplaced. Permanently.

Jealousy can cause a person to do some vicious things. I can't help it if no one ever wanted her recipes.

March, 1991

The hurrier . . . oh, stick it in your ear!

There used to be a little slogan that was tacked on the walls of small service businesses, such as shoe shops or the dry cleaner's or some similar one-man or Mom-and-Pop business. Perhaps you've seen it. It said:

The hurryer I go, the behinder I get.

Believe it. Truer words were seldom spoken.

Last week sometime marked three months that we have lived in this house that we hope will be home for a long time to come. You sure can't tell it by looking.

"In a few days," relatives and neighbors assured us, "you'll have that house looking like you've been there all your life."

Sure we will.

The house looked better the day the moving truck pulled away than it does now. Then, at least, everything still was in boxes. Stacked boxes look neat. Partially unpacked boxes, as many still are today, do not look neat. They look junky.

Now you must understand that this house was in really good shape when we moved in. Excellent repair. Clean as a pin, as they say, although it's never been really clear why they say that.

But did you ever see a woman move into a house and accept it just as it is? No change whatsoever? C'mon, whom are you trying to kid!

Let's start in the living room, which is close to three times as large as the old one in Alabama. The carpet's got to go, she said. It's quality carpet, in good shape. But the color just isn't right, she explained so convincingly.

It will be just right in the downstairs family room. But first, we had to have some book shelves and cabinets built in. Former newspaper guys squirrel away a lot of old papers and ex-teachers never part with a book.

A couple of weeks, a lot of sawdust and a dollar or two later, the woodworking project is finished and the carpet has

48

been moved to the basement, which from this moment on will be known as the den, said the woman who cleans it. Why not office? Or library? That would sound really classy and perhaps scare away some visitors.

Anyway, that project cleared the way for new carpet in the barn . . . uhh, living room. The nondescript color, which can be described as neutral at best, blends in well with everything else, so, with a little luck, carpet shouldn't be part of our vocabulary for the next few years.

Then there were some projects that were begun in Alabama. Stripping and refinishing of a twin bedroom suite, a china cabinet and a night stand. That work was followed immediately up here by refinishing of another bedroom suite, two more night stands and a folding door to go where there wasn't one but perhaps should have been.

And we really should do something about the shower in the master bedroom, shouldn't we? It may be all right now, but it'll need some work in a year or two, so we might as well do it now. It'll cost more the longer we wait.

Now, who can argue with logic like that? The ceramic tile man finished up just a few days ago.

And some pretty wallpaper border on these white walls will look as if the entire room has been redone. Heaven knows what will be next.

Meanwhile, 10 to 15 boxes of who knows what still sit in the garage, waiting to be unpacked. Fifteen or so boxes of books finally have been placed on the shelves. Two or three had already been opened on the chance that something urgently needed just might be in that particular one. No such luck.

The golf clubs haven't been out of the bags since fall of 1987, except for one driving range visit in Florida last spring. When last seen, the fishing rod had been broken down and stuck into a golf bag for safe packing. They're all better off where they are.

There's still so much to do. But we're not hurrying. We're far enough behind already.

July, 1989

What would we carry in a gun rack?

Living in the South for almost six years gave opportunities to do a lot of things folks don't do up here near the top of the map.

Right before we left, for instance, some friends gathered for a good riddance fish fry. People in the North fry fish too, but not on such a grand scale or with the frequency that Alabamians do.

They practically pull the plug on the nearest and biggest lake

49

and it's every fish for himself. Don't even ask what kind they were. The only fish we're even casually acquainted with are cats or gold.

Whip up a batch of hush puppies and french fries, and dig in. Fish and barbecue are the southern way of life.

Another thing we'll miss is frequent trips to the beach—every weekend if we kept up our school and house work.

We took in a Mardi Gras. Not in New Orleans, however, but in Mobile, Ala. Mobile's celebration, although not as big, naturally, is even older than New Orleans' and not nearly so crowded.

And just how many Buckeyes or Kentuckians do you reckon ever went to a rattlesnake roundup? There's one every February in Opp, Ala. We conveniently found something else to do every spring when it was time for the chitlin' festival at Clio.

We were introduced to, and enjoyed, boiled peanuts. A neighbor explained that you simply get a big batch of peanuts right after they've been plowed up and allowed to dry for a few days, put them into a big kettle of salted water and boil them. How long?

"It may sound smart alecky," he replied, "but you boil them until they're done. You'll know when they are."

If you never have eaten boiled peanuts, here's a tip: You probably won't like them. But they sell a lot more boiled peanuts at baseball games in the South than they do roasted ones like you eat at Riverfront Stadium in Cincinnati.

Still, there were other things we didn't get to do or failed to accomplish, mainly because we left sooner than we originally expected.

For one, we never were able to grow respectable looking pampas grass. Neighbors had it, almost in every yard, its proud, feather-like plumes taunting our scrawny little green leaves that seemed never to reach maturity.

We couldn't figure out the problem. Perhaps it was because our grass cutter never would see it in time.

We never got around to owning a pickup truck, either. Pickup trucks are in every driveway—or front yard—in the South. A big, shiny luxury auto usually is the second car. Pickups are No. 1.

You see even young girls tooling around town in a flashy pickup, just as proud as if it were a Jag or one of those other fancy jobs. And there we were, in a plain four-door sedan. We were as square as the vehicle.

It was probably just as well, though. We wouldn't have had anything to put in the gun rack found in every pickup. A golf club, maybe, or a fishing rod, even though we really can't use either. No way could you carry a typewriter or computer in one.

June, 1991

Two little kids, one old grouch

Our elder daughter and her two children, a boy 4 and a girl 2, came up from western Kentucky a couple of weeks ago for their first visit since we returned to Ohio. That made us very happy.

After five nights, they left for home. That made half of us happy . . . well, a little bit, at least.

Think about it a minute or two before joining the woman who prepares my meals in stirring up a nice kettle of bubbling tar with a side order of tiny feathers.

There were five of us—and frequently two or three more relatives who live nearby—cooped up (trapped?) in a house that's still topsy-turvy from our recent move from Dixie. Actually, it was topsy when the young'uns got here, turvy when they left.

And nobody warned us this was the monsoon season in Ohio. You can only make a child play outside in the rain so long before the neighbors start reaching for the phone.

The head of the house did just fine, thank you. But everyone knows Grandmas are much more tolerant than their mates.

But consider just some of the following:

These two don't know the meaning of the word "no," particularly when their mother is speaking. Maybe it has something to do with the context in which it is used. They don't understand, "No, you can't dance on the coffee table." But they do know what it means when used in, "No, I don't want to eat that yukky green stuff."

They showed great promise of developing into a championship relay team. It will be a new event, perhaps in time for the 1992 Olympics, and it will be called the 10-yard screen door slam. The object of this race is to see which child can come in one door and sprint out the other with the least elapsed time between SLAM! SLAM!

In the experimental stage, this event was limited to two competitors. But the possibilities are limited only by Grandpa's patience. Or temper. They're interchangeable.

The younger one had the uncanny knack of turning off the TV at the exact moment the detective show plot was at its thickest or the news commentator was about to say what Pete Rose had called Bart GeehowdIgetintothis.

She also is well on her way to making alarm clocks obsolete. She lives on a farm and knows what it means when she hears a rooster crow. She still rolled out at a goshawful time every morning, even though the only roosters around here are fried or

51

frozen.

The garage floor was frequently (always?) covered with golf balls, baseballs, tennis balls and softballs and a future million-dollar athlete swung at them with a fly swatter. At least they didn't find the golf clubs or learn how to use the garage-door opener.

There was one thing missing this visit. On their last trip to Alabama, the 4-year-old made a bold stomping attack on a fire ant hill. He hadn't the slightest idea how fiercely they could retaliate; after all, fire ants don't live as far north as he does. Or as far north as Grandma and Grandpa do now, hallelujah!

That's enough, isn't it? At least this time the TV remote control didn't get lost in the Cheerios box.

But there were lots of fun times, too. Going to a flea market for the first time was something special, and Grandpa got a gold star for courage for being gutsy enough to take them by himself.

They enjoyed seeing the barges at Greenup Dam, but even that took a back seat to the playground at a nearby grade school. Going to the Golden Arches for a Dr. Pepsi was fun, too. That's what he asked for and that's what he thinks he got.

But the best time of all came at the end of tiring days (for all of us) when a couple of soft, freshly bathed youngsters, with that magical smell no perfume maker can ever hope to match, snuggle beside you for a good-night story.

It just doesn't get any better than that.

June, 1989

Forget wallpaper, slap on some paint

If the Good Lord had meant for walls to be papered, He wouldn't have invented paint. Or brushes, rollers, sprayers and any of the other things you use to spread paint.

Or paneling.

Still, some people choose to cover their walls with paper. Why is beyond me. It's difficult to match. It's sticky. You have to cut around door facings and windows and electrical switches and outlets. Sometimes it goes on crooked, and that's not always your fault. Sometimes it won't stick. Sometimes it even falls.

True, some of it is very pretty, especially in the big, heavy books they have stacks of in the wallpaper stores. Some of it is indescribably ugly. You wouldn't want to put it in your doghouse . . . unless you hate your dog. Or any other kind of outhouse, for that matter.

We have just finished a wallpapering job at our house. Two small bathrooms and one good-sized bedroom. Funny thing about that bedroom is that it seemed to get larger with every strip. It wasn't a really big job. People who know what they're doing probably would have finished it in a day at the most.

We knew what we were doing, all right, but we just don't know how to do it fast. We don't measure how long it takes us to paper in hours or days. We think in terms of weeks. And it doesn't take that many weeks until you're talking months.

It's not that we had never papered before. Both of us had papered walls before, as long ago as when you still made paste at home, out of water, starch and flour. That's why the finished job had bumps in it—lumpy paste.

Nowadays, all you have to do is sock it down in the bathtub or some other container of water and it's all ready to be stuck on the wall. If you'd have done that back in the starch-and-flour days, all you would have had was a strip of soaking wet paper ready to fall into pieces when you started brushing it to the wall.

But that was in the days when we were helping our mothers and we were merely go-fers. They did the important stuff; we'd go for this or that and clean up the mess.

The first time we ever tackled a papering job was back around 1960. It was a big room with some high ceilings, some low, some sloping. Lots of windows and doors.

The most important lesson we learned that time was never, ever attempt to wallpaper a ceiling again. When wallpaper doesn't stick to a ceiling and falls, it falls on you.

Almost 15 years passed before we tried again. Our memories had dulled and we had forgotten what a job wallpapering is. The only difference was by then the self-adhesive stuff was in use and we didn't have to make our own paste and smear it on the back of the paper.

Maybe that's why we decided to tackle the kitchen and dining room while we were living in Alabama a few years ago. Another reason could have been that the woman I paper walls with and I somehow had changed roles. For some inexplicable reason, she quietly had become the boss lady and I was back in the teen-age go-fer role.

That job was a piece of cake. It was one of the world's tiniest kitchens and the dining room was all open on one wall and the other three were practically all doors. The proverbial one-armed paper hanger could have done it without working up a sweat.

The switching of boss and go-fer roles really didn't have that much to do with it.

The Alabama project must have given us a false sense of our true abilities. We plunged into the most recent job as if we were a pair of pros. Another piece of cake.

That was the worst piece of cake I ever bit into. No way am I going into all of the problems and screw-ups. Seeing a grown man cry isn't a pretty sight. The tears might get on the new wallpaper.

We have a large living room that probably will need something done to it next spring. Wallpaper? Forget it. Move everything out of the room, cover the carpet and get out the paint. At least half of the people who live in our house finally has learned a lesson about papering walls. The hard way.

December, 1989

Water, water everywhere it shouldn't be

What you're about to read is not what I was about to write. Huh uh. No way. Not even in my worst nightmare.

Normally, at this time of year, I'd think of writing about trimming the tree. Why do lights always burn when you have them spread across the floor for testing, but don't even flicker once they're draped on the tree?

Or putting up the outside lights. Remember how nice and warm it was a couple of weekends ago? Great day to put up the outside lights, said the woman who helps me search for the extension cords. But did I listen? Noooooo. I'll be among the shivering, fumbling, grousing group of otherwise semi-intelligent males who wait until the temperature is well below freezing and the wind is nearing gale force to climb up on a teetering ladder and try to affix tangled strings of lights to an ice-glazed pine tree.

Or the task of addressing Christmas cards. Didn't so-and-so move last summer? What's the ZIP code for Timbuktu? You sure they didn't get a divorce?

But not today. This time I'm writing about water.

That's right, water.

Not the kind you drink or wash your face in. Or heat in a sauce pan to stir up a bowl of grits.

This is about the kind of water that sneaks up on you like a thief in the night and finds some way to enter your house and just mess up everything it can get to.

You remember how much it rained last weekend. Most of Saturday. Some more on Sunday. And it was still coming down on Monday.

We can't do anything outside, it was suggested, so let's put up the tree. OK, let's. That was about 2 in the afternoon. What seemed like years later, the tree was up. But not until, true to form, a string of 100 when-one-goes-out-the-others-continue-to-burn lights sparkled brightly on the living room floor but didn't give a single point of light once on the tree.

About eight hours and a leftover turkey sandwich after the tree came out of the box (forgive us, foresters, we really know trees grow in the woods and not in boxes), the assistant decorator announced he was throwing in the wreath and was going to bed.

But first he had to go downstairs and turn off the lights, the radio, the computer and everything else that was gobbling up kilowatts at a rate that makes Ohio Power Co. people extremely happy.

Downstairs goes by many names. Sometimes it's called a den, when we're trying to put on the dog a little. Other times, it's referred to as my library, even though there aren't nearly as many books as there once was. Or if I want to pretend to be a productive citizen, it's my office. What the heck, I have a computer, a typewriter, a telephone, a clock and a calendar.

Much of the time, it's only a junk room.

On this particular evening, it was more like an indoor swimming pool. And I can't swim.

Where did it come from? Who knows? We live high on a hill and the nearest water is in a faucet, not some kind of stream or river.

Who cares? Well, we do, certainly, because we want to take steps to see that it doesn't happen again.

Several days have passed. The car has sat outside because the garage is filled with everything that usually is in the den-library-office-junk room.

The carpet is 99 percent dry, thanks to some unsolicited but much-needed and appreciated help, a machine that sucked up water by the gallons, a couple of fans, an electric heater, a dehumidifier and a furnace that hasn't kicked off for days. Both Ohio Power and Columbia Gas should be tickled to death when we pay December's bills.

But it could have been much worse. Some people in the western part of the county suffered heavy damage or lost their homes completely. And a man lost his life over in Kentucky.

And think of the people who don't even have a home for water to get into.

Maybe we were the lucky ones.

December, 1991

4-Eat, drink and . . .

Hold it just a minute.

If a watermelon is seedless,

where do they get the seeds

for you to plant so you can

grow them in your garden?

Winter is best for gardening

The last weekend of February was just perfect for gardening. Winter gardening, that is. It certainly was no time for actually getting down and dirty, working in the soil.

That comes later, when the earth is warm and moist. When the turn of a spade can unearth enough fishing worms to make you seriously consider laying the tools aside and heading for the nearest lake or stream.

This wasn't that kind of weekend. No way. It was alternately sunshiny, overcast, blustery, snowy—from flurries with flakes so tiny they barely were visible to big, old wet and heavy ones that almost made you duck to avoid being KO'd by one.

Only one thing was consistent as the calendar's shortest month packed up and Marched away. It was cold. Very cold. Too cold.

It was a time to light a fire and sit before the fireplace and doze. And leaf through the seed catalogs that have accumulated in the last couple of weeks.

Let's see, there are seven of them, each filled with page after page of promises for the coming season. The reddest tomatoes, the sweetest corn, the greenest beans.

Actually, there were only six different catalogs; two were duplicates of the same one that weren't immediately recognized under the hypnotism of the crackling fire and the perfect garden.

You know it's going to be perfect when one of the wish-books promises:

"You and your family will enjoy the pleasurable hours spent in the garden planting, watching them grow, and then reaping a bountiful harvest of vegetables not available in your supermarket."

Think of the money you will save, not only by growing your own food, but also by eliminating the cost of entertainment. Who needs TV, movies, major league baseball (if and when)? Get the family together and go out back and watch the garden grow.

"Hey, Norm! Watch these suckers grow. That zucchini's three inches longer than when I started this sentence."

It doesn't take much to entertain some people.

Once you start picking, pulling, cutting and whatever else you have to do to gather garden goodies, you also have this to look forward to:

"You have never before eaten such scrumptious corn! Butterfruit flavor is not just super sweet; it is fruity, full-bodied and delightful in a way no other varieties approach. Melt-in-your-mouth tender kernels are plump, sugary sweet and juicy. They're a taste treat even when eaten raw!"

Notice, they use a lot of !'s in gardening catalogs.

Taste isn't the only thing promised for this year's crops. How does spineless, and therefore scratchless, zucchini grab you? That's the point—it won't grab you, not like that old spiny kind does now.

"Look, Ma!" the catalog calls. "No scratches! Now, harvest bountiful crops of high-quality, succulent zucchini without the itching and prickling caused by the sticky spines found on the stems of most zucchini."

Scratchless zucchini! What will they come up with next?

The catalogs already promise burpless cucumbers, stringless beans and seedless watermelons.

Hold it. Seedless watermelons? What do you plant to get seedless watermelons? The catalog offers a packet of 10 seeds for $2.95, but that price can't last very long. Just where in the world will they find more seeds if these melons are seedless. A crisis looms, for sure.

Forget melons and plant some yard-long beans. "A delicious green bean, as well as an interesting curiosity . . . this is the bean to have your picture taken with for the local newspaper." The editor will be tickled to death. The only possible problem is finding a basket long enough to hold them.

But my favorite is a sponge plant "that produces sponges and a delicious vegetable!"

"This rapid-growing, ivy-like plant has pretty flowers. When young, stuff and bake as you would squash. When fruit matures, peel the hard skin off and you have a fibrous good quality sponge for kitchen, bath and washing the car."

It won't be long now. Gentlemen (and ladies), start your digging!

February, 1990

Come on, garden, do your thing

It was a hot, sweaty, dirty job. But somebody had to do it. So we planted a garden, our first in at least 30 years!

Oh, there has been an occasional tomato plant or two over the years. Anyone can grow tomatoes. Just stick a plant in the ground out by the fence, water it and sit back and wait for the tomatoes to grow, big and red and juicy.

But it never seems to work out that way. We're still waiting. Something always happens that the seed and plant catalogs or the friendly folks at the greenhouse forget to tell you about. Such as worms that fell your plants without so much as a polite timberrrr! Or diseases that wait until your plants are like a pretty, yellow-flowering bouquet and then attack like a thief in the night and turn those pretty tomatoes-to-be into a wilted, withering vine on a stake.

But hope springs eternal, and so do gardens.

Now understand this from the beginning: This is no backyard garden with hardly enough soil to dirty your hands. This is a real garden, plowed and disked and everything else you do to a real garden.

How big is it? Biggg. Really big. This garden is so big that you measure it in achers, as in back, instead of acres. It's that big.

It's well planned, too. The first thing we did was sit down—that's always important—and decide what we didn't want to plant. You can eliminate a lot of stuff, such as work, that way.

Some of the first things we crossed off our imaginary list were pretty important garden staples. Potatoes, for instance. We won't be growing any potatoes, Irish or sweet. Carrots are out too, as well as beets, radishes—anything that grows underground. If you can't see it growing, forget it. That does away with the heartache of harvest surprises that occur when you dig into the hills (or whatever potatoes grow in) and there is nothing there. All of that greenery above ground was just a joke and the joke was on you.

Forget popcorn, too. We visited here last July when it was so hot those little kernels were popping right on the ears. We can do without that again.

Cucumbers, watermelons and other things that grow on vines take up too much room. So let's pass on them as well. On second thought, let's make one exception: zucchini. Anything as prolific and that can be served in so many ways as zucchini ought to be able to go a long way toward solving the world's hunger problem. We'll grow some zucchini.

Asparagus takes too long to produce. Rhubarb sounds too controversial. One head of cabbage will make enough slaw to last a year. Eggplants just may contain too much cholesterol. Artichokes are too dangerous and we absolutely will not attempt to grow anything we can't spell without carrying a dictionary to the garden, such as kohlrabi, cauliflower and broccoli.

That just about kept zucchini out, too.

So what are we growing? There's not a lot left. Some corn, Illini sweet, I think it's called. Blue lake green beans and some half-runners. We'll never be able to catch them. Butterbeans. And lots of tomatoes. The law of averages ought to let some of them survive.

There also will be two vegetables that are carryovers from our short stay in Dixie: peas and okra. Okra is a lot like zucchini—you can fix it a zillion ways.

The peas are another story. We're not talking those little round green peas that take up space next to your mashed potatoes; these are the kind of peas that every southerner eats at least twice a day. Black-eyed peas are a more common name for them, but there are also crowder peas and pink-eyed purple hulls. Honest.

Ask for pink-eyed purple hulls in Ohio and most store clerks give you a funny look and go on about someone else's business.

It was not a unanimous decision to grow peas. One member of the family, who once took three days to shell a hamper of peas any southern woman would have handled in a few hours, got real nasty about it. So she gets the job of scarecrow.

June, 1990

Culture shock in the supermarket

Adjusting to a new home in another state isn't all that tough. It helps, of course, when you have lived in the same town twice before.

But there's still an occasional run-in with culture shock.

It always happens when you least expect it. That's probably why it's called shock. Anyway, things go along real well for a couple of weeks, you finally remember your closest neighbors' first names—but not their children's—and you're beginning to feel comfortable.

You can go home again, you decide, contrary to what someone once said or wrote. Nothing's changed. Be it ever so humble etc etc etc.

Then something happens to remind you abruptly that things have changed in the last quarter of a century. People have changed. You have changed. Things aren't the way they used to be. And maybe they never were.

We found out just the other day how different Southern Ohio is from Alabama, even if we are in the southernmost part of this northern state.

We were fixing (not all of the South is gone yet!) to go to a covered-dish dinner and decided to take something we had acquired a taste for in Dixie. How about sweet-potato pie and a casserole built around that staple of nearly every Alabama meal, peas? Not those little green peas, mind you, but those known in the North as black-eyed peas.

That sounded good enough to the head of the house, so she sent her husband to fetch the fixin's.

It was easier said than done.

The sweet potatoes were no problem at all. All we needed and more too were available at the first supermarket we entered. The peas were something else again.

The first stop was the biggest store in town. Certain that it would be a waste of time to head for the produce department in search of fresh peas, we steered the shopping cart toward the frozen foods. Up the aisle, back down the aisle, then one more shivering trip. No peas. There were lots of those little green ones, but no black-eyed peas. Or, as our former neighbors in Alabama would have said, no real peas.

A very polite and helpful woman who worked in the meat department took a look too, then called the head of the frozen food department. No, he said, he didn't have any. And after listening to our description of what we wanted, he didn't seem too anxious ever to get any.

On to the next store. Same result, only worse. This store didn't have any frozen peas and it didn't have any in cans either. Even though no self-respecting southerner would ever even think of eating peas out of a can, we were getting desperate. And desperate times call for desperate measures. The young woman in this store at least knew what we were looking for, but allowed as how she had never eaten any and had no particular craving for them.

Third store: no peas. Just a blank stare from an employee who was convinced we were pulling his leg.

Back to the first store; surely it had some peas somewhere in all those aisles of canned goods. There weren't any among all the many kinds of beans. None on the shelf with the little green peas, either.

Then, jackpot! There were some right at the end of the aisle, the last possible place to look, squeezed in between turnip greens on one side and some kind of Nintendo cereal (honest!) on the other.

So we whipped up a sweet potato pie and our casserole with peas in it and, if we do say so ourselves, they were goooood.

There was only one little hitch. We were a week early. The dinner was the following week.

July, 1989

Report card time for summer's work

If it's all the same to you, let's keep this column a secret to be shared only by you and me. It's about that garden we (the woman I married, her mother and I) put out last spring, and I'd just as soon the county farm agent not know anything about it.

The extension service people, you see, put a lot of time and effort into helping people in agricultural pursuits. But if they found out about our garden, chances are they might just pursue us right out of the county.

No way will they learn its location from me. And even if somebody else squeals, steps already have been taken to plow under the evidence.

We just may have set gardening back a quarter of a century, which coincidentally just happens to be how long it had been since we tried our hand at it.

The snickers of the few relatives and friends (?) who saw the results of our plowing and planting weren't too bad. We understood that kind of stuff goes with the territory. Besides, they weren't going to be too smart alecky because they could see early on that they might be talking themselves out of some nice tomatoes or zucchini or even a beet or two.

What we're really concerned about is the possibility that the county agent might decide to take some kind of action to prevent the same thing from happening again next summer. He can't suspend our license, confiscate our hoes or anything like that, can he?

Here's a rundown of sorts on how our garden grew. It might not be appraised the same way the county agent would do it, but rather how an ex-teacher grades it. There won't be any F's, because any seed that worked hard enough to get out of the ground deserves at least a little credit.

SQUASH, ZUCCHINI, CUCUMBERS and other things that grow on vines: B-. Those babies really produced. We ate zucchini and cucumbers fixed every way possible except maybe smoked and we would have tried that if we could have figured out which end to light. The grade would have been higher, but all at once, it seemed, the vines just shriveled up and died. Are they supposed to do that?

GREEN BEANS: C (for a reason you'll learn later).

BANANA AND BELL PEPPERS: B. This grade could be higher, perhaps, but let's give them something to shoot for next year.

JALAPENO PEPPERS: C- (only because I'm trying to be a nice guy; cross me and it's a D.) Jalapenos are supposed to be hot, fiery hot. These wouldn't even make you think about water, let alone drink a glass.

TOMATOES: A. Beautiful. Plentiful. Delicious. Red ones and yellow ones. If everything else had produced nothing, the tomatoes alone would have made this little project worthwhile.

BEETS: A. Did we really plant beets? If so, why? Are beets good for anything besides maybe making a salad bar colorful? Obviously, I'm going to find out because those things did as well below ground as the tomatoes did above.

OKRA: C (for the same reason as green beans).

RADISHES: B. I think. To be honest, I don't remember. But a usually reliable source said they did very well. I'll take her word for it.

PEAS: C. These are field peas, that staple from southern gardens, not those wimpy little English peas. We had beautiful, healthy, green vines, but not a whole lot of peas. They really had no reason to produce. When we moved back north, as we crossed the Alabama line into Tennessee, the woman I married declared,

"I'll never shell another pea in my life." The peas were shocked out of a year's growth.

CORN: I (for incomplete, naturally). That's what you give a student who doesn't complete his or her work. Our corn started, but never finished. It just stood there and did nothing.

WEEDS: A (only because my old grading scale didn't allow for pluses after A's.) If everything had grown like the weeds, this garden would have been farm agent's dream. The weeds didn't give the green beans and okra—or the gardeners—a fighting chance.

"That's not weeds," declared the mother of the woman I married, "that's grass."

Not in my book. If you can't eat it, it's weeds.

September, 1990

The man knows good food

I have learned my lesson. Finally. But good.

After 37 years of putting words on paper (a computer screen or whatever was available), five-plus years of attempting to teach college students how to do the same and a year and a half of puttering around with a column, the message was loud and clear:

Be careful what you say about people. Choose your words carefully. Show a little compassion for your fellow man. (And fellow woman, too, although I'm not sure I know very many fellows who are women or women who are fellows, either.)

Now this doesn't have anything at all to do with libel or invasion of privacy or any of that legal business that can get you into deep trouble.

You learn that early; like the first day or two on the job. You learn it or you don't have a job very long.

Editors can get real huffy about a lot of things—typographical errors, misspellings, misplaced modifiers, poor sentence structure, dangling prepositions, split infinitives, pronouns that don't agree with their antecedents, all kinds of English things.

But they get huffier about libel and invasion of privacy than anything that is misspelled, misplaced, dangling, split or otherwise mangled.

I didn't libel anyone or invade anyone's privacy or any of those other things. What I did do was this:

About six weeks ago, I wrote a column about a member of this community who shall not be identified this time around. His initials are ALA, as in a la mode, a la carte, a la king, ALAbama, words such as that. His occupation will not be divulged. He is a civic-minded man who has done much for this community in the few years he has been a part of it.

63

So, when I wrote about him a little earlier, it bothered him somewhat. He even grew a beard, apparently in hopes he might not be so easily identified.

I made fun of the way he talks—as if he had a mouth full of honey . . . or grits. Looking back, I know I shouldn't have done that.

I belittled his place of birth, and where he was raised. He can't help it if where he was born cars and pickups, especially the latter, are plastered with bumper stickers saying things like "American by birth, Southern by the grace of God." (Sometimes that's all that holds the vehicles together.) I know it isn't nice to dig at someone's roots; ALA wouldn't have done that to mine.

And there were some other unflattering comments, all written with tongue in cheek but the results were akin to foot in mouth.

Did ALA get mad? No, sir, he didn't get mad. Instead, he got even.

First, he consulted some experts. Their identity has not been determined, but there has been some talk of involvement of the Alabama Mafia. Hey, if you've lived there, let me tell you just the thought is frightening.

His expert consultants decided that after 16-plus months back north of the Ohio River, I obviously was exhibiting withdrawal symptoms.

Withdrawal from the South, that is.

To remedy the situation, ALA invited me to lunch last week. No burger and fries for this lunch. No chef's salad or pantywaist quiche or finger foods, either.

With much help from the folks at a Second Street eatery that will also be unnamed (because it might be construed as a free plug and also because it might not want to serve such a meal again), we pigged out on:

Country ham. Fried apples. Grits. Turnip greens (or mustard greens or collards; I never did learn the difference.) And biscuits, with butter and honey.

This was the kind of lunch you take your coat off for and let the crumbs fall where they may. I learned my lesson, all right. What I learned was this: The next time I want a good Southern meal, exhibit some withdrawal symptoms and write another column about ALA (and use his real name, of course.)

The man knows good food and also where and how to get it!

September, 1990

Vidalia onions: The rest of the story

Darn. Double darn.

Please pardon my foul language, but that's exactly how I

64

feel. And I feel that way because, once again, facts have messed up what for years was a good story.

This particular story, which I first heard about a dozen years ago when we lived in the Deep South, was that those big, tasty Vidalia onions grew only in the shadow of the water tower of little Vidalia, Ga.

There was no reason to question that. After all, Vidalia could have had a very large water tower, even if it is a town of just a little more than 10,000 mostly good people.

So I didn't question it. Not until the other day when I picked up a Vidalia onion bearing a little sticker that asked: "Any questions? Call 1-800-Vidalia."

I did. A young woman named Mandy answered the phone. I had every intention of keeping the call brief, even though it was an 800 number and wasn't costing me a penny, until I heard that sweet, southern voice. I was calling about onions, but I was talking to a real Georgia peach.

My very first question was about the water tower. She shot it down immediately. Not the water tower, just the story.

"There are 13 counties that can grow and sell the Vidalia sweet onions," she explained politely. "Vidalia is just one of the small towns that started with it."

Mandy wasn't even in the shadow of the Vidalia water tower. She was sitting in an office at Bland Farms in Glennville, about 20 to 25 miles from Vidalia. Glennville is smaller—"but not that much," Mandy said—than Vidalia, which means its water tower shadow is probably smaller, too.

Onions are Mandy's employer's most famous crop, but not the only one.

"We have a lot of different products," she said. "We sell peaches and tomatoes and we grow soybeans and different things like that."

I wasn't really interested in soybeans and things like that, but I loved listening to Mandy talk. If I ever pick up a soybean with a sticker that invites calls to 1-800-Soybean, I'll probably call—hoping to get Mandy—and ask some probing questions about tofu.

How big a crop is onions in and around Vidalia? In just three grocery stores the other day, I found stickers bearing the names of eight different growers. You just have to know there would be several times that many in 13 counties. Six of those eight boasted that the onion I was thinking about buying was sweet. The other two simply assumed I knew that.

"We just ship the month of May," Mandy explained, "and then the weather gets too hot and we store the onions in controlled-atmosphere buildings and then when the weather cools down in September, October and November, we ship again.

"When we're not shipping onions, we have a catalog full of

jar products made with onions and different cakes and products like that which we sell."

I really should have ordered something.

Mandy had an answer ready when asked why Vidalia—or Glennville—onions have such a good, sweet taste.

"It's the soil. A lot of times it has to do with how much water they get, and just different things like that."

There are many ways to prepare onions besides putting a slice on your burger or cutting them up in a salad or a bowl of soup beans, Mandy advised me.

"We do have a recipe booklet that we sell—"They Only Make You Cry When They're Gone"—it's 96 pages. That's all it tells you how to do."

How about that old romance-spoiler, onion breath?

"They're a lot different. There's still a little bit of the onion flavor, but not as much as the regular."

Do Vidalias ever make a person cry, other than when they're gone?

"Every now and then you'll run across a hot onion . . . they might not have got enough water in the field. It's not very often that you will find a hot one, but every now and then you might find one or two."

Not content with spoiling the water tower shadow story, Mandy also overturned another that I had accepted as the Gospel According to Lewis Grizzard, a Georgian and proud of it . . .

He had written several years ago that he had been given the secret for keeping Vidalias fresh. Put them into a pair of panty hose, he was told. Tie a knot just above the onion and then put in another and tie a knot and repeat the process until the panty hose are filled. The idea is to keep them from touching one another, which is one reason they go bad if you leave them stored in a sack.

"That is a good way to keep them," Mandy agreed, "but we recommend that you wrap each one up in newspaper or paper towels and put them in the refrigerator."

Indeed, that is a better way to keep onions. Who would want to dump out the onions every time she (or he) wanted to dress up and wear the panty hose?

June, 1994

Tomatoes: Red, yellow, green and fried

This is my favorite time of the year.

Not because of the weather, that's for sure. It's an unwritten rule around our house that we should never complain about the weather in the summer. Instead, we save our complaints until the winter.

Even during the last few weeks that have been so boiler-room hot no one should dare venture out of doors until well after sundown . . . no complaints here. But just wait until December, January, even February when the temperature dips down into single digits and below and icicles hang from our noses. That's when we moan and groan.

You see, when it's hot, you can always take off as much clothing as the law will allow in the search for comfort. But when it's cold, you can only put on so many layers and then you can't move.

Besides, weather that is so hot and dry that your lawn turns to straw and there's nothing left to cut can't be all bad!

But that's not what makes this my favorite time of the year.

What does is tomatoes.

Plump, luscious, juicy, delicious homegrown tomatoes. Homegrown is the key word. They can keep those grown indoors wherever it is they grow them. Hothouse tomatoes taste like cardboard. Or worse.

Red tomatoes, of course, are my favorites. But the yellow ones are tasty, too. And a friend out in the country grows some that are ripe when they're green. And vice versa.

It's all very confusing. They taste good too, but their color tends to complicate things.

How can you tell when they're ripe?

I asked the green tomato-growing friend: Say you set out several plants that will bear red tomatoes and a few more that will be yellow along with some of those strange green ones. If you forget which plants are which, how do you know when the green ones are ripe? How do you know they won't turn red or yellow if you let them hang on the vine a little longer?

He just looked at me with a grin that said, "That's the dumbest question I ever heard!"

Green tomatoes also stir memories of my dad. He was crazy about fried green tomatoes, even before that became a movie title. They were simple to fix. Simply dip them in flour or corn meal and fry them until golden brown.

They were pretty good, but most of the rest of the family liked our tomatoes red and ripe and sliced. But Dad picked them green and fried them before they had a chance to get ripe. It was usually well up in the summer before we ever found a red one hanging on the vines.

The woman who slices tomatoes at our house lives all winter, spring and early summer dreaming of a bacon, lettuce and tomato sandwich.

I'm not nearly so choosy.

If no one's watching, my favorite way to eat a tomato is pluck it from the vine, wipe off any dirt and take a big bite. A little messy, perhaps, but goooood. Some salt makes it much better, of course, but there never seems to be a shaker lying around in the tomato patch.

I've heard that some people put sugar on their tomatoes, but I don't believe it. Why would anyone ruin a perfectly good tomato by sprinkling sugar on it! That's worse than putting ketchup on your eggs.

We don't even have a tomato patch this year. There are two scrawny little plants growing among some flowering bushes, but neither is even mildly threatening to produce.

That's no problem, however. Everyone else in the world grows tomatoes, it seems. I heard about one rookie gardener who put out 100 plants and doesn't know what to do with all of the tomatoes now.

But tomato growers are always happy to share. It would be rude to say no, thanks, when they offer some. So I never do.

August, 1993

What's for supper? Fry a mess of greens

They may look like weeds to most of us, especially when we find them in our lawns and gardens. But they're a real treat to the people who know what they're looking for and how to cook them after they've found them.

"I'm just dying to get out and pick me a mess of greens," said a woman who's good at both the finding and the cooking. She's been doing it for the last 75 years, give or take a few.

Greens are plentiful this time of year, although one of the favorites—poke—may not be plentiful until about the middle of May. But there are plenty of others, including the dreaded dandelion which can be found in nearly everybody's lawn.

Here's a rundown of some of the things that greens pickers look for, as described by this real veteran:

Wild lettuce. Looks something like dandelions, but is sort of lacy and grows flat on the ground.

Watercress. There are two kinds, both of which grow around springs or running water. One grows slightly up from the ground and really is tasty. The other is flatter to the ground and is bitter as gall. Or is it the other way around? You'll ruin your greens if you get the wrong one in them.

Plantain. Short stemmed with oval-shaped leaves. Plantain and wild beets look much the same, but wild beets are more reddish. Both are good.

Dandelions. Everybody knows what they look like. Also makes tasty wine.

Mouse's ear. Looks like plantain, only smaller. Grows in a cluster.

White top. Looks like it sounds. Grows in a bunch; green

68

stems with shiny leaves.

Butterweed. Light green, long stem. Looks like wild lettuce.

Pepperweed or peppergrass. Red and lacy. Try to find it before the yellow bloom comes out. Hot as fire. You won't want much of this in your greens.

Poke. Grows on a stalk, white flowers, dark purple juicy berries and a poisonous root. You don't want any of that. What you want are the tender young shoots. Break off the stalks and it will keep growing.

Turnip tops. Find a turnip field where the turnips have remained in the garden all winter and cut the new tops off.

Some of you may also have heard of sour dock, crow's feet, bear paw and similar names, but we never got around to them. Some greens are called by several different names, depending on where they are being picked.

"You may not believe this," my greens-picker suggested, "but (the green leaves of) violets are good in your greens, too."

She also touted a few young, green elderberry leaves. "You'll never need a physic," she explained.

A word of caution: Picking greens may not be for everybody. There's a good possibility you may pick a mess of something that you will cook up and eat and spend half the night hugging the commode. Or worse.

Your best bet is to find someone at least in their 70s or 80s for expert advice. Talk to the right person and he or she probably will offer to go along with you. And even help you cook them. Not all greens pickers are up in years, but few younger folks know or even have a desire to know about greens.

"Neither one of my girls knows anything about greens," my source said.

Once you've got a mess picked, wash them good, put a little salt in the water and cook them until tender. Then drain them and put into a skillet with some bacon grease and cook for 10 or 15 minutes. Oldtimers used fatback or salt pork but in these days of ultra-strict diet watching, even bacon grease draws frowns.

Sprinkle some vinegar on them and your greens are ready to eat.

"Bake a pan of corn bread and you've got a good meal," this proven cook said. "If you need anything else, boiled eggs or stewed potatoes are good."

Wouldn't it be quicker, easier and simpler to go to the store and buy some spinach, kale, mustard greens or something in a can?

"A mess of greens is just delicious," I was told. "There's no comparison to what you buy."

April, 1995

5-The media

First, we had newspapers,
then along came radio and,
finally, TV. Put them all together
and what have we got? The
media! God bless (?) us every
one.

We're weirding our language

Puzzled by that whirring noise you seem to be hearing so frequently? Don't be. It's just your favorite—and probably toughest—former English teachers turning over in their graves.

They do that often these days . . . just about every time they look down—or up, as the case may be—and hear or read what's happened to the language they took so much pride in.

See! There's one of the things that set them to spinning. I was taught not to end a sentence with a preposition. I know better, but I did it just the same. I didn't do it because I wanted to set an example. I did it because I was too lazy to go back and rewrite the sentence in a way that avoids breaking a rule of grammar.

That is the reason for most grammatical errors: laziness. Or perhaps indifference. I guarantee you, I was taught better. Keep your eyes peeled (however painful that may be) and you may find all kinds of violations in the following paragraphs: split infinitives, dangling participles, even verbing.

You never heard of verbing? It's done a lot in modern speech and writing. It's done so often that my favorite comic strip, "Calvin & Hobbes," called attention to it the other day.

Verbing, Calvin explains, is the practice of using nouns and adjectives as verbs. His example was access, which became a verb in the computer age. But there are many, many more. Just a few that come to mind are site, impact, host and fund. Fund and its various forms are perhaps the most overworked. Nothing is ever paid for or financed anymore; it's funded. And you don't need money, you seek funding.

"Verbing weirds the language," Calvin astutely observes.

"Maybe we can eventually make language a complete impediment to understanding," Hobbes adds.

Verbing isn't the only way this is being done. There's also the use of gobbledygook, a word that became part of our vocabularies in 1944 and which means "wordy and unintelligible jargon." More recently, gobbledygook has been replaced by doublespeak. If nothing else, it's easier to spell.

One of the most offensive is revenue enhancement as camouflage for taxes.

Not too long ago, a Wisconsin legislator proposed that all references in state laws regulating bowling alleys be changed to bowling centers. Alley just doesn't sound nice enough. Why not? We have medical centers instead of hospitals, criminal justice centers where there used to be jails and even financial or money centers have replaced many banks.

Workers whose contracts have expired or otherwise are unhappy no longer strike. Instead, they take job action.

Riots have been replaced by civil disobedience.

71

Toilet paper is bathroom tissue, garbage dumps are sanitary landfills, swamps have become wetlands, prisons are called correctional facilities or institutions, garbage is solid waste, soap is detergent and instead of running the sweeper, I now use the vacuum cleaner.

What janitors or cleaning people used to do is now handled by environmental services employees.

Not all good English teachers are turning in their graves. They're trying to do something about it. William Lutz, a professor of English at Rutgers University, has written a book titled "Doublespeak." The National Conference of Teachers of English gives a Doublespeak Award to the worst offenders. The competition is fierce.

"Doublespeak is not a slip of the tongue, or language used out of ignorance, but is instead a very conscious use of language as a weapon or tool by those in power to achieve their ends at our expense," Lutz contends.

How else do you explain:

Dehired or non-retained for workers fired or laid off.

Terminal living for death.

Hair disadvantaged for bald.

Calvin was only half right. "Verbing AND doublespeak weird the language."

February, 1993

A fond farewell to USA YESTERDAY

The self-proclaimed "Nation's Newspaper" is no longer my newspaper.

My subscription to USA TODAY ran out a few days ago, so I no longer find it in my mailbox every Tuesday through Saturday.

I knew this was coming. It was no slipup on my part, such as forgetting to get a check in the mail when the first of several reminders was delivered. I was well aware this day was coming. The handwriting has been on the wall (It's been so long since I last used that cliche that I just had to!) since early last winter. That's when the woman who writes the checks at our house for such things as newspapers, doctor bills and food and drink surveyed the clutter—mostly piles of newspapers—and declared:

"I think when USA TODAY runs out, you shouldn't renew it. You get all these newspapers and never get them all read. You've got all of these shelves filled with books and you never read any of them. You bought all of these books so you could read them when you retired. You've been retired five years and still haven't read any of them."

I meekly agreed, pointing out, however, that yes, I have read some of them. I have read all of the ones written by truly great authors such as Lewis Grizzard.

She's right, of course, as usual. We do get a lot of newspapers. We get three daily newspapers, not counting the late and lamented USA TODAY, semiweekly, a weekly, two college newspapers, two alumni newsletters and three magazines. Or is it four? Whatever.

So I didn't even put up a fight about dropping USA TODAY.

I would have if I found it in my mailbox Monday through Friday, the days of publication, instead of Tuesday through Saturday as mentioned earlier. That's a day late, for crying out loud, and you know what they say about yesterday's newspaper. If you don't, I'm not going to tell you because that's another cliche and I've already used this week's quota of cliches.

I've read the paper daily for 10 of its nearly 12 years of publication. It would have been longer, but the paper was two years old before daily delivery reached Cincinnati.

But when we moved to Alabama, I made an amazing discovery: I could subscribe for mail delivery and get the paper on the same day. It was put into my mailbox about 11 a.m. We'd walk home at noon for lunch and the paper, along with assorted bills, would be waiting.

"You better put that down and get a move on," the woman who ate lunch and walked back to school with me said daily. "You have a 1 o'clock class, you know."

Yeah, I know, I know.

Our paper arrived daily because USA TODAY has printing sites in Atlanta and nearby Gainesville, Ga. From either plant, the papers could be hauled to the post office, trucked down the interstate and beat me home for lunch.

But not so in Ohio.

The nearest USA TODAY printing sites are in Mansfield, Ohio, and Richmond, Ind., just about the same distance as the Georgia presses were from Troy, Ala. But the mail doesn't get here as quickly as it did there.

Oh, I'll still read USA TODAY—or USA TOADY as we derisively called it when I worked for one of its parent firm Gannett newspapers—every chance I get, such as when I find one someone has left lying in a restaurant or when I'm traveling and the motel provides a free copy.

Every once in a while, I might even let loose of two quarters and buy one from one of those funny-looking vending machines. But not every day; that's too expensive for a second (third, fourth or fifth) newspaper that arrives a day late . . .

And that's what it is, of course. USA TODAY can cram a lot of information in those four brightly colored sections, more perhaps than any other and that's why its daily circulation is higher than any other general interest newspaper in the country.

But it can't tell me anything about my hometown. Never has. Except for a deadly prison riot that was reported nationwide, I have to read my local paper to know what's going on here.

One more thing. For several months, USA TODAY has been collecting what I suspect is a lot of dollars for a U.S. Postal Service ad in the upper right ear of the sports section cover every day. That means a few of my tax dollars paying for that ad and helping put out the newspaper.

Wouldn't you think the newspaper and Postal Service could use a few of those dollars to figure out how to get the paper here on the same day it's printed? Is that asking too much? I think not.

May, 1994

It takes a whiner to know a whiner

I have a crow to pick with Andy Rooney.

You know, the guy with the bushy eyebrows who's responsible for the last four or five of TV's "60 Minutes" on Sunday nights.

Andy usually follows Mike, Morley and Ed or one of the others who do the longer exposes—also frequently referred to by their victims as journalistic hatchet jobs. Maybe, maybe not.

He comes on right before the Mailbag segment and the seemingly endless and nearly impossible to read credits to entertain us with "A Few Minutes with Andy Rooney."

It's my favorite part of the show. I may pick up a piece of the Sunday paper, sneak into the kitchen for a quick bite or hustle upstairs to the bathroom while one of the Messrs. Wallace, Safer or Bradley are putting the heat on someone. But when it's Andy's turn, I turn the volume up, tell the woman I watch television with to be still for just a few minutes and then I sit back and enjoy.

Andy's voice isn't all that great, not nearly as pleasant as the others on the show. There may be a better way to describe it, but the adjective I usually think of is whiny.

A whiny voice is perfect for what Andy Rooney does, because what he does is complain. And whine. He complains about all the things the rest of us would like to complain about if we had a TV camera and microphone to complain into.

You name it, Andy has complained about it. If he hasn't, he will. And we sit in front of the tube every Sunday evening, nodding in agreement and egging him on.

He has complained about how things are packaged, the size of metropolitan Sunday newspapers, cold remedies, junk mail, doctors, computers, repairmen, advertising . . . the same things we all complain about or would if we thought it would do any good.

One of his most sensible complaints was voiced many years ago about the sizes of men's clothing.

"I wear a size 8 1/2 shoe but I wear a size 11 sock," Andy said in one of his essays. "Does this make any sense? On the same foot?"

No, it doesn't make any sense at all.

Which brings me to my complaint addressed to Andy. It's about his books. He has written six of his own and collaborated with another writer on three more. I have all six of Andy's, none of the other three. The earlier ones had to do with World War II, which (thank God!) was just a few years before my time.

The six I have really are just collections of his essays. They're timeless and extremely entertaining. Some are even downright informative.

My complaint has nothing to do with the books' contents. What I'm griping about is their size. They won't all fit on the same shelf.

Books by the same author simply have to be on the same shelf. You can't have two on this shelf, two on another and two more on a shelf on the other side of the room. That would be a poor way to run a library.

I can get "Word for Word," "Sweet and Sour" and "A Few Minutes with Andy Rooney" on the same shelf. The first two are 9 1/4 inches tall and the third is 9 3/8. They fit perfectly on the shelf I had chosen for authors whose names began with R, S, T etc.

But "And More Andy Rooney," "Pieces of My Mind" and "Not That You Asked" are all 9 1/2 inches tall. No way can they be squeezed into the shelf without tearing the dust jacket or damaging the binding.

Wouldn't you think all of Andy Rooney's books would be the same size? Think of all the paper that could have been saved by making all of them just a tiny bit shorter.

Don't suggest that I adjust the size of the shelf. Change one and they'd all have to be changed. Then none of my books would have fit on any of the shelves.

Perhaps I should have complained to the carpenter who built my shelves instead of to Andy Rooney. But Andy is in New York and the carpenter lives just a few miles away. Close enough to hit me with a hammer for complaining.

February, 1994

From ashes . . . to ducks?

People send me clippings. They see something in a newspaper

or magazine that they think I may be interested in, clip or tear it out and the first thing you know, it's in my house. It may be a clipping about something they think I might want to write about or something they know I'd like to read.

I get clippings from all over. Some come from my children, although not nearly as many as they could send. They know I like to get them, and they know their mother is tolerant . . . up to a point. When the accumulation of clippings reaches that point, they know, as do I, that hell hath no fury like a woman whose house is cluttered from top to bottom with newspaper clippings.

I also get clippings from a former co-worker in Cincinnati where we lived for a long time, and also from a good friend who winters in Florida and sends me columns she clips.

But the one who outdoes them all is another former co-worker who now lives in Florida and works for one of the supermarket tabloids. What a fertile field for offbeat clippings. He sends so many clippings to so many people that he has to make copies. Every two or three months, he assembles a sizable collection of clippings, puts them in book form in a folder and spends about a buck and half on postage and puts them in the mail. He can't possibly imagine how much I enjoy them.

What do I do with clippings? Most of them are in manila folders or four accordion-type files with alphabetized pockets. They don't cause me any problems whatsoever. The ones that do are the clippings I leave on the night stand, my dresser, the coffee table or the tea cart that sits between the chairs we occupy when reading or watching TV. There they frequently reach, even pass, my children's mother's tolerance limit.

Perhaps that is why I seldom can find a clipping that I find a need for after weeks, months or possibly years.

The most recent clipping to come into my possession came from a very good friend who is a frequent contributor. Titled "Thoughts on the Business of Life," it offers thoughts about newspapers from 14 writers ranging from Thomas Jefferson to Henry David Thoreau and including the likes of Ogden Nash. It's a keeper for sure, if only I can remember where I file it.

But I'm puzzled. The clipping—an entire page, actually—is from Forbes magazine. Until now, I had no idea that I even knew anyone who subscribes to Forbes. It couldn't possibly have been torn from a magazine in a doctor's office or barber shop; it was dated March 17, 1995, at least a year or two too current to be in one of those places.

Another clipping contributor brought me one three or four years ago touting "the ultimate gift for the sportsman on your list who is no longer able to enjoy hunting or fishing because he has, unfortunately, kicked the bucket."

There's this place in Des Moines, Iowa, you see, that you can send the cremated remains and "they will, for a price, load the ashes into a shotgun shell, take the shell on a hunting trip and shoot it at a duck or other game animal of your choice."

Or, if you prefer, the ashes will be placed into a fishing lure or a duck decoy. Think about it; the possibilities are unlimited.

Who would do such a thing? you may be asking about now.

Paper-clipped to the first article is a second that appeared in USA TODAY about a year later. Below a small photo of at least 10 shotgun-wielding North Carolinians, there was the brief report of the send-off given one of their cronies who had recently departed for that Great Hunting Ground in the Sky. Each of the mourners was given two 12-, 16- or 20-gauge shotgun shells containing their friend's ashes. Following a few words by the man's daughter, the shooters pointed their guns skyward and pulled the triggers.

Keep those clippings coming, folks!

March, 1995

'Eyes have it, no, the 'Ears recover

The TV announcer's enthusiasm, excitement and home team partisanship fairly leaped right into the living room.

"It's the Ears' ball, first and 10 at midfield with a chance to score before halftime and . . ."

Wait a minute! What did he say? Who in the wide, wide world of sports are the Ears? And where did they come up with a name such as that?

It just goes to show you can't snooze, read the papers or any of perhaps a half dozen other things you tend to do when you really don't give a hoot about either of the two teams the network has decided you WILL watch today.

The team on the tube wasn't really the Ears. No school would name its sports teams the Ears.

The Ears were simply the product of a trendy broadcaster who had shortened the name of the West Virginia University football team.

He wasn't saying Ears. What he really was saying was 'Eers . . . as in Mountaineers. Get it? That's how the in crowd talks. And certainly sportscasters are part of the in crowd. Sportswriters are, too.

They toss around sports slanguage, punctuated with cliches, that no Joe or Jane Phann can understand.

You have to be an announcer, writer, coach or perhaps a player to have the slightest clue what they're talking about. They tend to forget that the whole Phann family is none of the above. This Ear or 'Eer business started in Florida, home of the 'Canes and the 'Noles.

Those aren't real names, of course. 'Canes is the in-the-know way of talking about the University of Miami's Hurricanes.

And 'Noles, as anyone who spends his or her lifetime in a press box or locker room would know, is how to impress the average Phann that you know all about Florida State's Seminoles. What's next? you ask.

How about the Ohio State 'Eyes? Makes as much sense as 'Eers. And, continuing in the Big Whatever-Number-It-Is-Now, you could find the Indiana 'Siers, Michigan 'Ines, Michigan State 'Tans, Minnesota 'Phers, Wisconsin 'Gers and Penn State 'Ions.

North Carolina's Tar Heels already have been abbreviated to the Heels. Does this sports name shrinkage mean they soon will be simply the Eels?

Silly, isn't it? Let's just call a spade a spade, an 'Eer a Mountaineer and the 'Eyes an only slightly better than mediocre football team.

These aren't the only sports names in the news these days. The end of the World Series hasn't silenced Native Americans' unhappiness with Jane Fonda, the tomahawk chop and the use of tribal names as team monikers.

No less an authority on Atlanta, the South and grits than columnist and author Lewis Grizzard has wondered in print if the Braves still will have that name on their uniforms come spring training.

And much pressure is being put on the Washington Redskins to ax or otherwise get rid of that war-like symbol.

But perhaps the Braves and Redskins are misunderstood. Maybe they don't mean anything at all disparaging by using what appear to be Native American names.

Two things justify Atlanta's use of Braves: the city's traffic and Underground Atlanta. You have to be a ferociously Brave to tackle either.

As for Washington, what goes on in that city on the Potomac is enough to make anyone's face red. Permanently.

November, 1991

Lewis and Lucy and the good old days

Lewis Grizzard is just about the best newspaper columnist to put words on paper. He has this way about him, you see, that makes you feel like he's writing for you and you alone.

Never mind that just about everyone in Atlanta reads him. That's his home territory, where he fills himself on corn bread and barbecue and a cold one now and then. Anyone in Atlanta who doesn't read Grizzard probably just reads The Wall Street Journal or one of those pretend newspapers and don't know what real writing is.

And never mind that his column is syndicated from here to there and back. You can pick up a paper in Troy, Ala., Portsmouth, Ohio, or Ironton, Ohio, and there's old Lewis's column, written real personal and folksy like, so people can understand it. Many major metropolitan papers, particularly in the North, don't carry Lewis because he isn't politically correct. That's their problem.

Not very many columnists write like that. You read them and then you wonder what'd he mean by that? So you assume it must have been important and good or the newspaper wouldn't have let him have all that space.

Lewis can write about anything. He can write about his Mamma or his departed Daddy and make your eyes a little watery. He can go to Moscow and write about Russians. He can write about Southern cooking and make you feel stuffed. He can write about stuffed shirts and pseudo-intellectuals and make you say out loud, "Yeah, Lewis, right on. Give 'em hell."

Grizzard is one of the South's real treasures. Although his column is syndicated all over and his books sell nationally too, it wasn't always like that. Five years or so ago, you could ask for a Lewis Grizzard book in a Cincinnati bookstore and the clerk would just look at you kind of funny.

It's different in the South. When Lewis gives a talk there—you'd never call one of his talks a lecture—people come out to listen. In about six years at Troy State University down in South Alabama, only two things filled the auditorium to capacity—spring commencement and Lewis Grizzard.

And Lewis has class, too. Name one other person who can come on stage wearing a pair of Gucci loafers and no sox and not get snickered at. That's it! He never takes himself too seriously.

What all of this is leading up to is a piece Grizzard did a couple of weeks ago in tribute to Lucille Ball. Surely you read it on this editorial page. He said what he had to say about Lucy and he said it well, as he just about always does.

He said one more thing: "But I loved Lucy, too. Maybe I loved her time even more. It will never be that way again."

No, it won't. And more's the pity.

Do you know there's an organization whose sole purpose in life is to keep you from thinking about and enjoying the good old days?

Well, there is. It calls itself the National Association for the Advancement of Time. The very name sounds like a put-on, but it probably isn't. It probably is an honest-to-goodness organization that takes itself far too seriously, just like most such groups.

Its co-founder was quoted in USA TODAY a month or so ago: "The USA is mired in a tar pit of nostalgia. This obsession with the past is a drain on our country and our culture. As a people, we cannot move forward until we cast off the dead weight we drag behind."

Well, that sounds good. But if it's all the same to the time advancers, things haven't advanced all that well in recent years. We look around and see how things are in 1989 and it's no wonder we would rather wallow in nostalgia.

At least we know what the '50s and '60s brought. Then things started going downhill in the '70s and '80s and heaven only knows what's ahead in the '90s.

What have we got to look ahead to? The greenhouse effect? Another disastrous oil spill? The ozone layer going to pieces? Some madman pushing the button on the big one?

No, thanks, give me an extra large helping of nostalgia and go a little heavy on the Lucy. Grizzard's right, you know. It will never be that way again. But at least we can remember.

May, 1989

Far too many TV miniseries

"Anything good on TV tonight?" the woman I watch the boob tube with asked.

I don't hear that question very often, because we don't watch TV that much. Really. We seldom watch daytime offerings. We turn the "Today" show on the few mornings we get up early (well, not really early but kind of if you consider 7 early; I do) except when the weather is bad. Then, we turn on the radio to see if its too snowy or icy for old codgers to be out.

We never watch what's on between 9 a.m. and 5 p.m. Newton Minow most likely never dreamed of shows such as Phil, Oprah, Sally, Geraldo, Jenny, Jerry, Ricki, Maury and Montel (I hope I haven't left anyone out) when he was Federal Communications Commission chairman back in 1961.

That was when he took a long look at what he described as "a procession of game shows, violence, audience participation shows, formula comedies about totally unbelievable families, blood and thunder, mayhem, violence, sadism, murder, western bad men, western good men, private eyes, gangsters, more violence, and cartoons. And, endlessly, commercials—many screaming, cajoling and offending."

"A vast wasteland," Minow labeled much of television programming.

That's what the man said and he was talking about TV in 1961—more than 30 years ago! What would he say if he were broadcasting's czar in 1995?

Would you believe, perhaps, "a vaster wasteland"?
Perhaps.

So now you know why we don't watch a whole lot of TV at our house. We turn it on Mondays for CBS's comedy (?) lineup that is capped off by the ever so bloody "Chicago Hope." Like NBC's similar hospital show, "ER," "Hope" doesn't show us a whole lot of violence—just what the violence produces. We try to catch "ER" when we can because its star, George Clooney, attended Northern Kentucky University when I was teaching there and his father, former Cincinnati newsman Nick Clooney, is an old friend. (Name dropper! Name dropper!)

I also like "Seinfeld," "Home Improvement" and "Coach" when they're not on opposite a University of Kentucky basketball game. But my spouse doesn't share my enthusiasm for any of those shows, including UK, except for maybe "Coach." I think she's got a crush on Luther.

So when she asked, "Anything good on TV tonight?" I gave her the usual answer, "The same old same old." That meant "60 Minutes," which already was down to about "45 Minutes," and "Murder, She Wrote," which seems, to me at least, to be losing it since Jessica has fled scenic Cabot Cove and is traipsing hither and yon to help local cops solve murders that otherwise would go unsolved.

"Then," I continued, "you have your choice from among 'Dances With Wolves,' 'Children of the Dust' and 'Op Center.' I said "your" choice because all three of them are miniseries."

She knows I have an unwritten but frequently spoken rule about miniseries. I never watch them. Ever. Not even "Roots," the granddaddy of all miniseries, which was on two or three months, as I recall. I did watch the first part of a miniseries about 15 or 20 years ago, but I can't remember the name of it. That miniseries was so interesting, so gripping that we completely forgot to turn on the set the next night. There's only one show that I'll watch night after night like a miniseries. That's David Letterman. The monologue, the Top Ten List then it's lights out.

"I don't see why you can't watch one of them with me," Mrs. Miniseries insisted. "You sit and watch one basketball or football game after another and they're all just alike."

"Oh, no," I begged to differ, "they're not. Right when 'Dances With Wolves' gets interesting, when Kevin Costner is about to fall in love or ask a wolf to dance with him, the show will cut off and you'll have to wait until tomorrow night to find out who fell in love with whom and who danced with what.

"But I promise you this: The first time I'm watching UK and Rodrick Rhodes goes driving toward the basket or Tony Delk launches a three-pointer and a commercial comes on and someone says the game will be concluded tomorrow night, I'll quit watching basketball. Rodrick can drive only so far and Tony can hang in mid-air only so long."

And to tell you the truth, I bet Kevin Costner isn't all that crazy about waiting so long to dance with a wolf. I bet he hopes the show gets pre-empted. Or even canceled. But it wasn't and she watched it. I didn't.

March, 1995

I can't remember what I forgot

They say (whoever "they" are) that memory is the second thing to go with advancing age. I forget what the first is.

"They" probably are right.

It seems that I have been forgetting a lot of things lately. So many that I can't remember them all.

Just last week, an organization my wife and I belong to was supposed to sing our national anthem prior to a basketball game. I forgot to tell my wife. It didn't really make that much difference, because advance warning wouldn't have improved her singing at all.

But that's just half of it.

All of us singers were supposed to show up wearing blue shirts. Nearly 75 did. Two showed up in gray shirts. Guess who.

These aren't isolated incidents. I write this weekly drivel on a computer in my home. I can't send it to the newspapers on a modem because I am not bright enough to learn how to use one. I hope to. In fact, I have hoped to for six or seven years. Maybe longer.

So what I do is take a computer disk to one newspaper, mail the so-called hard copy to two others. Simple enough? Not quite.

More times than I care to remember I have driven to town, came within a block or two of the newspaper office and then driven home with the disk still lying beside me on the console. And the letters to be mailed still on the back seat. We have driven past four post offices, once going and once coming home.

The woman who reminds me of things I have almost forgotten tries to help. She isn't overly successful. Her assistance was prompted by my cutting clippings from newspapers and magazines for future reference. But I always forgot where I put them.

"What you should do," she suggested, "is get a manila folder or a large envelope. When you cut something out, put it in the envelope and you'll know where it is."

It sounded like a good idea. Not necessarily brilliant, but worth a try. I got a manila folder out of the filing cabinet, which I have been cleaning out since October, and on the outside wrote in heavy, black letters: **Check this folder every day.**

I even double underlined **every.** I should have used two or three **!!!**s, but apparently I forgot.

82

It worked for a few days. Then she grew tired of the folder messing up the organized clutter on the table between our chairs. It was banished to my den. I looked in it about 5 minutes ago. The latest clipping in it is dated October, 1995. I must have forgotten the day.

So much for good intentions.

Little sticky notes (I can't say Post-it notes because that's a registered trade mark and its owner gets fussy about such things) that you stick on the refrigerator and other places visited frequently don't help. Most of the time they fall off and sail under the fridge, never to be seen again unless the ice maker quits working and the repairman comes calling.

I have a friend who teaches a memory course, like yesteryear basketball great Jerry Lucas was famous for. But Jerry's greatest claim to fame, besides leading the NBA so many years in rebounding, was memorizing things such as the New York City phone directory. That's no help if you don't know anyone in New York City, which I don't.

Now, let's see, what were we talking about before we got to basketball . . . ?

P.S.: This column was an hour late getting to the newspaper office. It was written in plenty of time, stored on the computer disk and placed on the kitchen table where it wouldn't be forgotten. But it was just the same.

February, 1996

6-On the road again

There's a song out with
a line that goes something like
"wherever you go, there
you are." Just make yourself
at home.

Four wheels or I'm walking

Until the 12th month of my 63rd year, I had managed to survive quite well, thank you, without ever getting into or onto a motor-propelled vehicle with fewer that four wheels.

Correction: I seem to recall some sort of motorized two-wheel conveyance a friend of mine owned when we lived in one of the Northern Kentucky suburbs of Cincinnati. It was manufactured by the French, I believe, and I rode out the street a couple of blocks and back at a speed just sufficient to keep the thing from toppling over.

Of course, I was a youngster in my 30s and quite wild and reckless then. But I had sense enough to know even then that if the Good Lord had meant for us to ride on fewer than four wheels, He wouldn't have created Ford, Chrysler and General Motors.

That enabled me to remain in one piece, unscratched, unbruised and unbloodied. Until just a few weeks ago.

We gassed up the motor home—which has six wheels—and headed north into Wisconsin, home of a couple of old friends who were our neighbors 40 years ago. He was an ironworker who came to Southern Ohio to help build a new blast furnace at the steel mill and, later, the atomic energy plant up the road a piece at Piketon.

These people, man and wife alike, love the outdoors. They also love motorized vehicles that help them get around outdoors without walking.

On their property were the following vehicles: seven snowmobiles (of absolutely no use when we were there in August), two three-wheel all-terrain vehicles, a couple of motorcycles, a pickup truck, a sensible sedan and various and sundry tractors, including a John Deere with a front-end loader. Everything in season was gassed up and ready for our riding pleasure.

I was offered a spin on a three-wheeler, which you may recall was banned from further production several years ago in a rare burst of bureaucratic intelligence. Like any red-blooded American dum-dum, I hopped on and was ready to rumble. My host was explaining what to him was the simple operation of the bright yellow contraption and turned on the ignition.

In approximately three to five seconds at most, the three-wheeler and I parted company. Abruptly. Painfully.

I hit the ground harder than I ever had hit it before. If there had been a Richter scale anywhere nearby, it would have registered between a 2 and a 3. Maybe higher. I'm sure of it.

The three-wheeler would still have been going until it ran out of gas, toppled over somewhere or smacked into one of the millions of towering pine trees. Instead, the big green John Deere tractor was parked conveniently and directly in the three-wheeler's path. The runaway contraption ran right into the loader and halfway up the tractor, coming to a halt only inches short of toppling backward onto my already aching and prostrate body.

Nothing was broken. Everything was badly shaken. No shaken isn't strong enough; make that jolted. The only visible damage was an egg-sized knot on my bleeding right shin.

Our host, who feared he had killed someone he hadn't seen in four decades, looked as if he were on the verge of a heart attack.

For three days, it was all I could do to climb into my over-the-cab bed in the motor home each night. It was even more painful to remake the bed the next morning.

That was eight weeks ago, and there are still occasional aches and pains where I had never ached or pained before. The knot on the shin is only marble sized now.

And all of my modes of transportation forevermore will have at least four wheels.

October, 1994

Butterflies and other migrants

The passenger to my right had been chattering nonstop for nearly four hours, which wasn't the least bit unusual. You get used to it after nearly 44 years. The only thing different on this particular day was her topic of conversation: the cotton fields on either side of Interstate 65.

"Isn't that beautiful?" she asked for the eleventeenth time in the little more than 200 miles we had traveled through the northern edge of Tennessee and the heart of Alabama. "I wish we could stop and I could climb through the fence and pick a handful. It looks just like a fresh snowfall. Isn't it beautiful?"

Eleventeen plus one. And counting.

"I don't remember seeing cotton this far north, do you?" she babbled on, forgetting to pause long enough for an answer. "We usually see it around Montgomery, but I don't remember any cotton in Tennessee or north Alabama."

She had a point there. I couldn't remember as much cotton as we had seen on this day, and never more than just a few miles to the north of Alabama's capital city. Of course, it could have been because we hadn't been north of Birmingham in the last five years. We had been leaving I-65 there and traveling I-59 toward Chattanooga where we hooked up with I-75 for the drive north.

Perhaps those fields have been filled with rebounding King Cotton for the last few years. Who knows?

Suddenly, she changed the subject.

"What was that?" she asked. "Something orange and black

just hit the windshield."

The colors were appropriate. After all, it was just a few days before Halloween. And something orange and black had indeed hit the windshield and some of whatever it had been was still there.

It looks like a butterfly, I commented. Or, at least, what's left of one.

"Oh, I remember," recalled the woman I watch butterflies flutter by with. "Those are monarch butterflies. I read a story about them in the paper this morning. They're on their way to Mexico."

Why in the world are they going to Mexico? I wondered aloud. Seems to me that it would be simpler just to winter in south Florida. They could go down around West Palm Beach or even Miami . . . On second thought, I guess those monarchs know what they're doing.

We continued to see monarchs the rest of the way to Florida's Panhandle beaches. Sometimes, they resembled swarms. Other times, there were just two or three making their way to winter quarters outside Mexico City—providing the trip didn't end on a car or truck's windshield or grill.

At Destin, we found Monarch Festival 1994, a month of field trips, garden tours, lectures and a few things, such as sidewalk sales and German food, music and dancing that didn't really have anything to do with butterflies. There was, however, a $60-per-person garden party and dance to raise money for the festival's conservation efforts.

Monarchs aren't the only things heading south for the winter.

Also migrating are:

Hummingbirds. These tiny overachievers travel even farther than the butterflies. Better taste in destination, too. They head across the Gulf of Mexico to the Yucatan Peninsula. And why not? That's where Cancun is and Cancun has Mexico City beat hands down.

Canada Geese. Don't call them Canadian Geese. They get very upset when called Canadian Geese; so do Canadian people. Perhaps that is why Canada Geese honk so loudly and make such a mess if they poop on your car.

Snowbirds. Some snowbirds fly south and nest in condominiums for the winter. Others travel and reside in large and expensive recreational vehicles. Hostile natives often greet them with bumper stickers and/or window decals that say: 'I DON'T GIVE A DAMN HOW YOU DO IT UP NORTH.' But they always smile when they extend their hands for damn Yankee dollars.

November, 1994

Just hangin' out on Saturday night

It was just like many other Saturday nights in Vanceburg, Ky., a wide spot in the road about 75 miles east of Cincinnati, the nearest metropolis.

It was raining, as it does so often in late November. Not really hard, though. Just enough to get you wet if you stayed out in it very long.

And foggy. That's not unusual either in Vanceburg. The fog comes rolling up from the Ohio River and settles in, making itself right at home.

Two police cruisers were keeping the streets hot. They crisscrossed the nearly deserted town, looking out for those who may have tipped a few too many or were otherwise misbehaving.

Not many people were out. For one thing, it was really the wee hours of Sunday morning. For another, most traffic nowadays stays on the Double A Highway a mile or so away and is headed for Portsmouth, Ohio, Maysville, Ky., or points beyond.

A flashing blue light from one of the cruisers knifed through the fog, telling everyone still up that someone had been caught doing something against the rules.

Over in town, the busiest place was the all-night convenience store and service station with the laundry next door.

A few cars pulled in for a couple of dollars worth of gasoline or to fill'erup. The store had hot coffee or cold Cokes. College sweat shirts at a good price. Lottery tickets. Sandwiches. You name it. Just another Saturday night turning into Sunday morning in Vanceburg.

But one thing was different. Very different. There was an unusually large number of people just hanging out at the all-night convenience store, service station and laundry.

And these people didn't look like the usual hangers-out. For one thing, just about everyone was wearing royal blue sweatshirts that proclaimed to the world these people were from Shawnee State University across the river in southern Ohio. And you could count on the fingers of one hand those young enough to be out and about at this time of the night. The rest should have been in bed hours ago!

These people, who proudly call themselves the Golden Bears, all had boarded a chartered bus early Friday morning to go to Nashville, Tenn. Their main purpose was to watch Shawnee State's women's basketball team play in a tournament. But they also squeezed in a quick visit to the Opryland Hotel and other sights that tourists like to see.

They had a ball. Never mind that their Lady Bears basketball team lost both games. The Golden Bears cheered the girls and jeered the referees, just like any loyal fan would do.

Then they started home, the Lady Bears' bus close behind.

Somewhere along the way, some electrical problems developed on the seniors' bus. Its lights grew dimmer. When the driver stopped to call for assistance, the team bus unknowingly passed and continued on to Portsmouth.

As the lights grew dimmer between Maysville and Vanceburg, the passengers became quieter. The wisecracking was replaced by whispered prayers. The loud, mostly off-key singing gave way to soft, peaceful hymns.

In Vanceburg, the driver pulled off for a final time and called again for help.

It was a little more than three hours before a replacement bus arrived.

The Golden Bears made themselves right at home. They're good at that; they've had so many years of experience.

The men mostly stood around out front, telling tall stories. They were interrupted once by a man young enough to be their grandson and who had emptied a few too many bottles or cans. He zeroed in on a man whom he recognized as "the old coach" and challenged him to get his team together.

The women settled into seats in the laundry. One young woman was washing clothes and keeping an eye on a cute, little blonde about 2 years old who ran among the washers and dryers, a little puzzled by so many Grandmas smiling at her.

One of the nicest things the Grandmas did was to give a few reassuring bear hugs to a definitely down-in-the dumps young driver. He needed that.

Finally, about 3, transportation home arrived. It had been another fun time for the Golden Bears, just hanging out on Saturday night in Vanceburg.

November, 1992

These oranges left a sour taste

CLERMONT, Fla.—The sign was lettered crudely in handwriting that appeared to be as shaky as the roadside market it stood before:

"ORANGES
$2"

That's all. No indication of how many. It could have meant $2 a bag. Or it could have meant $2 apiece or $2 a ton. You never know.

"Stop!" called a voice somewhere to the rear of the driver's seat. "Let's get some of those oranges."

I can't, the driver explained. This is a divided highway, they're on the other side, and this traffic is terrible.

Besides, he continued confidently, there'll be zillions of other stands just like that. Why buy them now and have to haul them all over Florida for three weeks?

Good answer. There were, indeed, zillions of other stands . . . well, perhaps not zillions but at least a half zillion.

Fortunately, for the driver but much to the chagrin of his citrus-starved passengers, most of them were on the wrong side of a divided highway. Or they were closed. Or there didn't appear to be anyplace to park an RV.

You had a glass of orange juice for breakfast, didn't you? That ought to be enough for today.

Nearly three weeks passed. In spite of a half zillion roadside stands up and down the peninsula—all of which were on the wrong side of divided highways—the only taste of citrus came from frozen juice purchased in Ohio. And a few hard-to-chew orange slices that must have been survivors from Christmas.

The passengers to the rear of the driver's seat were becoming desperate when we stopped to refuel not very far south of Jacksonville. This was no longer citrus country. Next stop: Georgia, the peach state.

"Look at that sign!" called the same voice heard earlier. "Those are even cheaper that ones we saw a couple of weeks ago. Let's go get some."

She had seen a huge billboard that said:
"INDIAN RIVER ORANGES
$1 BAG"

The sign was colorful and neatly lettered. The market was large, clean-looking and busy.

Allllriiiight! the driver agreed. Oranges are messy and sticky and squirty, but you can't beat that price. Go get 'em!

We didn't get any oranges. Unless you count three small slices offered as free samples.

The woman who buys and peels all the oranges at our house walked from one end of the market to the other, then retraced her steps. She found oranges for $5.98 a bag and she found oranges for $7.98 a bag. She did not find any oranges for $1 a bag.

"Where are the oranges for a dollar a bag," she asked a worker.

"Two oranges for a dollar," he answered, reaching for a paper bag. A small paper bag. "What do you want for a dollar, lady?"

That did it.

"Well," the angry orange shopper responded, "that sign is just a big come-on. You get people in here, then tell them two oranges in a bag. I'll get mine up north.

And that's exactly what we did. Navel oranges, 10 or 11 of them in a bag for $2.99. They came from California, too. Nya!

Nya! Nya!

April, 1992

Getting there in plenty of time

The first clue that perhaps everything wasn't as it should be came at the front desk of the motel in Goodlettsville, Tenn.

"We don't have a reservation in that name," said the once-upon-a-time young woman behind it. "Is that your first name or your last name?"

Until then, everything had been as smooth as the miles and miles of newly resurfaced highways paid for by "Your Tax Dollars At Work."

It was going to be a great trip, we just knew it. How could it be otherwise when Lexington, Ky., service stations were charging only $1.039 for the same gasoline that was going for $1.189 back home?

There wasn't a cloud in the sky. Temperatures had cooled considerably overnight. Traffic was light. The Double A Highway had been easy to find at Quincy, Ky., and even though the new road still had no identifying signs, it quickly delivered us to the Bluegrass Country leading to Lexington. From there, the drive on U.S. 68 with its miles and miles of horse farms was a sight for sore eyes.

This was an almost spur-of-the-moment trip. That's the nice thing about being old and almost over the hill. You wake up (if all went well during the night) in the morning and if everything is in working order and there is no surplus of aches and pains, you just go where you want to go and do what you want to do. Within reason, of course.

A few days earlier, the phone had rung. The excited voice on the other end told us a couple of our neighbors were going to be playing at the Opryland Hotel in Nashville with their band, "South Point."

Would we like to go? Silly question.

Of course, we would. Besides, the boys are family. Kissing cousins. First cousins twice removed. Or maybe its second cousins once removed. Whatever.

At any rate, it turned out that "South Point" had been asked to play at the fourth annual Major Independent Record Awards Show.

That's not all. "South Point" had been nominated for best new band and was a finalist. Hey! the band members, relatives and friends thought, this could be the break "South Point" has been working and waiting for. And as kissing cousins or whatever, the least we could do was give moral support.

But that woman at the front desk who didn't have any

reservations in our name—first or last—also didn't have any for "South Point" or in the name of our cousins.

Oh, Lord, we're at the wrong motel and we don't have tickets for the show and what in the world are we going to do?

A cooler head prevailed. The woman I sometimes check into out-of-town motels with called the Auto Club or somebody to check on the reservations. Somewhere during the conversation, the desk clerk overhead a name she recognized and started checking names and dates again.

"Yes, here we are," she said so sweetly and efficiently. "But they're for next week."

Next week?!? Do you mean we drove 350 miles on the wrong day?

Yep, so help me Conway Twitty, that's exactly what happened. How dumb can a person be? (That's a rhetorical question and you're not supposed to answer it.)

Are we going again on the right date? Possibly. Probably. After all, we've already run through a dress rehearsal. Both ways.

June, 1991

Dream vacation was only a dream

Oh, what a vacation this was going to be!

The planning had started half a year ago—'way back in September when thoughts were about raking leaves, football . . . fall things.

But every couple of weeks, something would arrive in the mail to remind us of what awaited just around the corner of the new year. Brightly colored brochures in Florida colors of pink and coral. There even was a video of people just like us who had fled the frozen north to find poolside relaxation in the tropical sunshine . . . blazing colors of sunset . . . an evening of romantic moonlight dancing.

Stop! Not another word. We're too old for stuff like that.

Finally, January passed. February was short. March arrived. It was time to head south. We would leave early Saturday morning when traffic was lighter. Stop for brunch somewhere in Virginia and spend the night around Columbia, S.C.

Sunday would get us through Georgia, we would stop for a free orange juice at the Florida state line, spend a few days in the West Palm Beach area and then continue on to Fort Lauderdale. There, we would board a luxury ocean liner with lavish buffets and proceed to that paradise the brochures and video had been telling us about.

Yeah, sure.

That was before we started reading, watching and listening

to weather forecasts. We were in for the mother of all blizzards, the weather watchers advised.

Maybe if we leave on Friday, we tried to convince ourselves, we can get ahead of the storm. We'll put the pedal to the metal (or is it the metal to the pedal? it's hard to understand what those truckers are saying on the CB radio) and outmaneuver that nasty old storm.

After all, we were on our way to a sun-drenched, action-packed adventure of a lifetime! We were going to have seven days and six nights to find our own paradise. We could bask in the sun, sip our favorite tropical drink, shop at exclusive boutiques, play blackjack at exciting casinos or just walk on a secluded moonlit beach.

That's what the brochures and video said.

What we did was shiver in the snow, sip coffee or hot chocolate, play Uno or solitaire and walk out to the wood pile and get a few more logs for the fireplace.

The day we were supposed to be in South Carolina, we were sitting at home looking out the window at snow. We were there, too, when we were scheduled to be at West Palm Beach and Fort Lauderdale and on the boat. Six months of planning and I'm still not sure exactly where we were going.

You see, I'm not all that crazy about water unless it's in a glass or a bathtub. Or maybe frozen in little cubes, cooling something that tastes good.

We're still snowed in at home.

Maybe we can leave Tuesday, we told ourselves. The roads will be clear by then.

In our dreams.

The first thing we heard Tuesday morning was that I-77 was still closed at the Virginia border. Can't go that way.

There's always I-75, we decided, even if we don't like to drive an RV through Atlanta. I-75 is still closed at the Tennessee-Georgia border, the friendly voice at the Auto Club advised us. We kind of expected that. They're still embroiled in a 20th century war between the states when it comes to snow removal.

The man at the Ohio Highway Patrol was even more emphatic.

"Haven't you been listening to your radio?" he asked. "They don't want you coming into the South. I-75 is closed, traffic is blocked and they're turning people back."

Can't go that way, either. We just can't get there from here.

Surely, the roads are open by now. But we're still in Ohio. Because our boat sailed without us.

March, 1993

93

The real reason people stay in motels

It had the makings of a beautiful autumn weekend. It turned out to be what more accurately could be called the camping trip to hell.

OK, maybe it wasn't quite that bad. In fact, we've had many weekend outings that were much worse. You know, things such as flat tires or mechanical trouble on the camper, never-ending rain, sick kids, electric outlets that didn't work, cold water in the showers or even no water at all.

But you try not to think about horrors of the past. After all, it had been five weeks since our last outdoors jaunt. Time was growing short. It soon would be time to winterize the camper and think instead of fireplaces and other things that you can enjoy without leaving the house.

Our destination was Fort Boonesborough State Park, just a short drive south of Lexington, Ky. It's our favorite campground in Kentucky, a place you can go and know you will enjoy it.

Instead of just two of us this weekend, there would be six—ranging in age from 6 to 80. The camper will sleep six, the manufacturer's literature assures us. But it becomes a little snug. Maybe we should make other arrangements.

I know! How about borrowing the next door neighbors' tent? It looked really neat when the girls had a slumber party last summer.

Assured by our neighbor that the tent was really simple to put up, off we went to Boonesborough.

There are a lot of chores to do when you arrive at a campground, things that should be and were done before we attempted to put up the tent. Go back a few words and underline attempted.

It may be simple to put up, as we had been told, but we were even simpler. No way were we going to get that thing off the ground.

Help arrived. A nice, old Kentuckian camping nearby sauntered over and assured us he knew how to set up the tent. It took only a few minutes to see that he knew even less about tents than we did.

More help arrived. A young park worker driving a golf cart drove up to the pile of canvas and confidently assured us he would help erect our extra bedroom. A short time later, he shook his head in frustration and hopped back into the golf cart.

"There must be someone in here with a tent like this," he called over his shoulder. "I'll be back."

He returned with a young man who called everybody "Sir." He grabbed both hands full of canvas and aluminum tent poles and went to work. He was no more successful than we first three failures.

Just when we were ready to put it all back in the duffel bag, a comic strip light bulb went on over the young man's head and he saw the light. He got the tent assembled, with the help of five others, and declared:

"It'll stay up all right, but there must be a piece missing."

It did stay up and we did find the missing piece. It was in our next door neighbor's garage.

Our troubles were far from over. Assembling the tent was a piece of cake compared with inflating the air mattress that would make the tent livable. We huffed and we puffed before someone discovered there were two plugs, not just one, that had to be in place before the air would stay inside.

The next day was better, but not much. The refrigerator didn't work properly. The front wheel on a bicycle locked and had to be half-carried back to the campsite. The nice, old Kentuckian who knew so little about tents did know a little about bikes. He got it to rolling again.

Oh, I almost forgot. It rained off and on both days. We became used to that back in the days when we used a fold-down camper and many a time had to pack up wet. That experience came in handy on this outing. The grandson who shared the tent with me has problems if he drinks too much shortly before bedtime. As a result, we had to pack up wet again.

November, 1993

95

7-This is progress?

Isn't modern technology
wonderful? We have call
waiting, call forwarding and
can hit a computer key
and file all our work on that
Great Floppy Disk in the sky.

Wanted: small all-purpose opener

There is one word that I would like to direct today to all of the manufacturers, marketers, packagers, promoters, distributors and anyone else who plays a role, large or small, in supplying us with all the products we encounter in everyday life:

GIMMEABREAK!

This plea is directed not only to those devilish people who put those two little crackers in those impenetrable cellophane packages we find on salad bars or that come with a bowl of soup. I solved that problem long ago.

I have a 12-inch pair of shears that became expendable several years ago when newspaper folk quit typing their stories on long sheets of copy paper and the wire services turned to computer monitors in place of printers that spewed out the news of the day on endless rolls of paper. Scissors went the way of typewriters, paste pots and eyeshades in the newsroom.

But I found a use for mine. The woman I eat out with now carries them in the small suitcase she calls a purse. When we help ourselves to the crackers, I reach for the scissors and SNIP! The crackers are open before my soup is cold or the lettuce goes limp.

I'm not selfish. I'm more than willing to pass my scissors around to others struggling to get their crackers open. And they appreciate it; you should see the looks on their grateful faces. We do draw the line, however, on diners who use my scissors to cut up their spaghetti. Especially if they've already dipped up the sauce and sprinkled the Parmesan . . . That makes an awful mess in a purse.

The scissors also come in handy in opening packets of sweetener or the little mint placed on the table at the end of the meal. But they're no help at all with the butter, margarine, jelly. Those little containers are not meant to be opened under any circumstances. Unless you just happen to be carrying a very small stick of dynamite. Forget it.

Recently, however, we discovered another area where the manufacturers, marketers etc. (see first paragraph above) conspire to drive us to early insanity.

The woman I share a bathroom with lined up seven containers of perfume, cologne and other things that smell good. Each of them had at least a half inch of liquid remaining inside, and one was half full. But there was no way to get it out and onto the skin you love to touch and smell.

Either the spritzer wouldn't spritz or the little plastic tube was too short to reach the last of the stuff that we paid far too much for in the first place.

"No problem," I declared. "I'll get some tools and get it for you. I'll take the tops off the bottles and you can pour it out in your hand like I do my after shave."

Silly me.

There was only one tool that would have worked on those little bottles: a ball-peen hammer. But one not-so-gentle tap with the hammer and there wasn't a drop left inside. There wasn't much bottle left either.

Another product that doesn't give you everything you paid for is underarm deodorant.

There is always at least a quarter inch of it left in the dispenser that you can't get to. You can rub it under your arms until the plastic container takes the skin off, but there will always be at least a quarter's worth you can't get out.

So what if the package promises to provide 24-hour protection, keep you fresh all day and not to stain your clothing? It can't do any of those things if you can't get it on.

My 12-inch shears are no help at all with this packaging problem.

The only thing left to do if you can't get to your perfume or deodorant is to raise a big stink.

February, 1995

No wife means no phone ringing

My wife left me the other day.

Not permanently . . . I don't think. But I should know for certain in a week or so. Her original intention was to grab a few days of R&R—along with a few rays—at the beach. Never mind that she left with a younger man; that was her brother. She also was chaperoned by their mother, and a handful of other relatives was waiting when she got there.

So really what my wife left me the other day was peace and quiet. Unbelievable peace and quiet. Peace and quiet like I have known very few times in the past, and then only for a few hours at a time. A day and a night at the most.

You see, not only was her voice removed from the house, so were numerous others.

The reason was simple (and should be obvious): The phone rang only one time! Can you believe that? Just one phone call. And that was you-know-who informing me that she had arrived you-know-where safe and sound.

What had been suspected for oh, so many years became oh, so obvious during that peacefully quiet time: The worst intruder on peace and quiet is the telephone.

There probably are a few reasons why we have to have phones. For one, someone has to help the electric company pay for all those ugly poles that clutter the neighborhood. And if we didn't have the poles, there wouldn't be any place to hang the

TV cable.

So we have to have phones. Remember when Woody Hayes (God rest his soul) used to say three things can happen when you pass the football and two of them are bad? That applies to phones as well.

A lot of things can happen when your phone rings. Most of them are bad. It can be a wrong number interrupting dinner, an interesting TV show, a nap or some other pastime. It can be one of those recorded telemarketing calls that you can't interrupt. All you can do is hang up and that isn't nearly as satisfying as cussing out the idiot on the other end.

It can be a storm window or aluminum siding salesman.

Or it can be your mother-in-law.

There are other telephone distractions, too.

Perhaps the worst is call waiting. I think that's what it's called. I wouldn't know for sure because we don't have call waiting. We also don't have one of those things that kick in after a couple of rings, tell you that no one's home and if you want to leave a message, do so after the beep.

We don't have call waiting or an answering machine and we're not about to.

We don't like to be talking to someone on the phone, hear a little beep and be told, "I have another call; hold on and I'll be right back." How long is "right back"? Just long enough to hang up and leave the phone off the hook for the rest of the afternoon and/or evening.

Personally, what I would like to have is call forwarding. We had it at one of the newspapers where I used to work and it was something like this: If you knew you were going to be away from your phone for awhile, you could push a button and program your calls to be forwarded to another phone. If you were smart, you didn't do that and you wouldn't have to answer the phone until you returned to your own.

Another alternative was to forward all of your calls to another area code. Do you think Ma Bell's son, Alexander, and his cohort, Watson, really had all of this in mind when they invented the phone? Surely not.

If either had the slightest inkling, this probably would have been the scene in Boston back in 1876 when their work was interrupted by Bell's spilling a container of acid into his lap:

"Mr. Watson," Bell yelled into the phone, "come here, I want you!"

"I'm sorry, I can't come to the phone now," Watson's recorded voice would have answered. "Please leave a message after the tone."

Or he could have forwarded the call to Cleveland. There were no phones there yet.

November, 1992

99

Number, please? All 35 or 36 of them

The telephone has been a remarkable (choose one: convenience, blessing, curse, pain in the ear) since Alexander Graham Bell (or was it really Don Ameche?) made his first call in 1876 and got a busy signal.

If only someone had called Bell-Ameche and given him a clue. If the inventor had known what he was getting us into, surely he would have hung up, tossed the contraption out the window and turned his inventive talents in another direction.

We would have been spared such things as caller ID, answering machines, call waiting, call forwarding and the most common of all, call losing.

None of that stuff existed when I was a kid. The most common problem then was "the line is busy."

The reason the line was always busy was that we didn't have a phone. So we went to the next door neighbor's or the grocery store down at the corner. After the second or third trip of the day, the neighbor or the grocer wised up and was quick to inform us "the line is busy."

For those of you younger than a half century, that was way back when only business places or the very wealthy had private lines. The rest of us shared a line and every time you picked up the phone, someone was talking and just about everyone else on the line was eavesdropping. There weren't many secrets in those days.

Some businesses had easy-to-remember single- or double-digit numbers. Party lines shared the same number followed by different letters . . . 47-A, 47-B and so on.

You didn't dial. You'd pick up the receiver and if Mrs. Whatshername wasn't spreading the latest gossip, the operator would come on the line and say "Numberrrr pleeze" and you'd tell her and modern—or, at least, current—technology took over from there.

Out in the country where I frequently lived, you didn't answer every time the phone rang. You answered only when it was your ring. If your number was 2911, for instance, the 11 meant a long ring and a short ring. If the phone rang two longs and a short or some other combination, the call wasn't for you so you didn't answer. Instead, you waited a few seconds, then very quietly picked up the receiver and listened in. Hey, we didn't have television then so you had to do something.

The reason I bring all this up is that a short time ago the woman I eavesdrop with was attempting to make some calls from Cincinnati. The instructions on the phone advised her to press 7 for an outside line, then 0, the area code and the number she wished to call. That would be something like 7-0-614-555-1234.

If you're keeping track, that's 12 digits so far.

Then you normally hear a melodic tone and a recorded voice thanking us for using AT&T and instructing us that if we're using a Touch Tone phone we should enter our calling card and PIN, which stands for something but I'm not sure what. That would be 614-574-xxxx-xxxx. That's 14 more digits; now we're up to 26. And we still could get a busy signal and have to do it all over several times because this phone was so old it didn't have a redial on it.

But it didn't work that way. Instead of the recorded "thank you for using AT&T," the voice at the other end said "Sprint." Or maybe it was MCI or Herbie's Telephone & Car Wash Co. But it wasn't AT&T. We wanted AT&T.

The woman trying to make the call almost had reached the point where she had forgotten whom she was calling and why. But she doesn't give up easily. Somehow, she found out that if she wanted AT&T, she had to call 7-1-800-321-0288. That would be followed by 614-555-1234. If all went well, then she would be told to enter her calling card number and PIN. That's either 35 or 36 digits; I get a different total nearly every time I count them.

Let your fingers do the walking? You have to be kidding! They're too tired. Whatever happened to two longs and a short?

April, 1994

Tax time causes ringing in ear

The phone begins ringing shortly after 8 a.m.

A phone should never ring that early, unless it's the network checking to see if Bryant Gumbel overslept or a kid calling the radio station to see if the morning's heavy frost means a one-hour delay or—please, God!—no school at all. Whoopee!

Eight o'clock only comes once a day at our house and that's in the p.m., certainly not a.m. We could unplug the phone, but that's too much work. The cord snakes around under the bed and you bump your head on the nightstand and nearly turn over the lamp and spill the glass of uhh . . . water waiting for you.

Then, in the morning, you have to go through the entire process in reverse. Only thing different is that the glass of uhh . . . water is empty.

That's too much trouble. It's much easier to leave the thing plugged in and just mutter nasty things about the @&*#!$@! who woke you up just to tell them they had got the wrong number.

It's always the wrong number. A friend would never call that early. Even a mother-in-law who firmly believes that phones were invented to be used continuously wouldn't call that early. She would call someone else who believes as she does.

We didn't use to get wrong numbers before we had dial phones. We'd simply lift the receiver and an operator who sounded and probably looked like Lily Tomlin would answer "Number puhlease" or "Central."

We'd give her something like a short and three longs or 1021-F or 35-X and she'd come back and say, "Sorry, that line is busy" and we'd mutter nasty things about the phone company and hang up.

Now everything is automated and we still get aggravating busy signals and more wrong numbers than Lily Tomlin ever thought possible.

We get so many wrong-number calls because when we moved to our new home late in April last year, the phone company assigned us a number that had just been surrendered by an income tax preparation service. Never mind which income tax preparation service. That would be free advertising. The first newspaper editor I ever worked for always reminded us, "You can't sell it if you give it away." I think he was talking about advertising.

Anyway, we got a few wrong-number calls in May and even early June. Some of them didn't sound overly happy. We just figured they either didn't get a refund or if they did, it wasn't as much as they would have liked. So it didn't help a bit when someone else answered the phone.

The phone—and we—got a lot of rest until a few days after Christmas. Then a few earlybirds who obviously expect to get a lot of bucks back began calling the last few days in December. Never mind that the tax preparation folks' new number is listed in the new phone book. People remember, and call, the old number.

Business has been picking up considerably through January and the first few days in February. In fact, income tax preparation might not be a bad business to go into if you know anymore about mathematics than how to spell it.

We've been running 8 to 10 calls a day lately. It's kind of frightening to think what it will be in April. That might be a good time to get out of town for a few days.

At first, it was tempting to simply tell callers, "Sorry, this is their old number. No, I don't know what the number is, but I'm sure it's in the book."

But because most callers were so polite and apologetic, the head of the house wrote the new number down near the phone and cheerfully passes it along even when not asked. I do too.

Oh, sure, the phone company probably would have given us a new number if we had complained and asked them to change it. But this is the easiest number to remember we've ever had. Why else would all those people remember it from last year?

We'll just keep the one we got. Things will quiet down April

16.
No deals. Unless the phone company can give us a short and three longs and throw in Lily Tomlin to boot.

February, 1989

Evening of TV made to order

You've probably heard the guy's commercial.

How did Abe Lincoln put it? You can tune out all of the commercials some of the time and some of the commercials all of the time. But if you have a radio or TV set, you can't tune out all of the commercials all of the time.

Maybe it wasn't Abe Lincoln. But he probably would have said it if he'd had cable. Anyway, this guy doing the commercial is singing the blues about how difficult it is to program his VCR.

Hey, we can identify with that, can't we!?! Never have so many tried to record so many TV offerings and had so little success.

It's not certain who said that, but it could have been Abe Lincoln if he'd had cable and a VCR to go with it.

Seemingly intelligent people attempt to program a VCR to record a certain program they're going to have to miss for any one of a zillion reasons.

Then they go on about their business. Later, they return home, push the rewind button, followed by play.

What happens? Nothing. Somehow something has gone wrong. Again. That's what happened to the guy on the commercial. Just as it does to you and me.

But he's had it up to here with the usual ways of setting the VCR to record his programs of choice. And he's not going to take it anymore.

"I'm not a dummy," he tells his vast audience. "I'm president of my own company (as if the VCR gives a diddly darn). But I can't program my VCR."

Then he proceeds to tell us of this new way of voice programming your VCR. (Do you suppose that could be the company he is president of? Of course not. He wouldn't stoop that low, would he? Well, maybe.)

"Just tell it to record Channel 5 on Friday, May 7, from 8 p.m. to 10 p.m."

I tried it, exactly the way he said to do it. Even bent over real close to the speaker and pronounced each word clearly. But it didn't work.

The next time the commercial was on, I listened all the way to the end. His last words were:

"Just call 1-800-XXX-XXXX for complete details."

That probably means you have to buy something (more than

likely from the company he is president of) to enable you to record whatever it is on Channel 5 between such-and-such time and such-and-such time.

But, look, if it works as well as he is trying to lead us to believe, whatever he's selling could be worth its weight in remote controls.

Not only could you have ordered it to "record Channel 5 on Friday, May 7, from 8 p.m. to 10 p.m.," but you could even tell it, perhaps, to "skip the commercials" or at the very least to "turn the volume down until the show comes back on."

Or "switch to ESPN and check the baseball scores."

Try it a few times to make certain you have the hang of it, then branch out.

Tell your machine, "Record Channel 5 on Tuesday, May 11, from 8 p.m. to 10 p.m., skip the commercials and at 9 p.m. order a 15-inch pizza with everything but anchovies, also a two-liter Pepsi."

If it works, let me know. I want to record a few shows, black out the commercials and enjoy a pizza. And maybe have whoever or whatever it is taking all those orders cut my grass during station breaks.

May, 1993

Some assembly may be required

Tell me this: Would it cost all that much more for manufacturers to assemble their products before we buy them?

The answer, of course, is yes. It would cost a bundle more. Why? Because that's just the way things work. Any excuse anyone can find for marking up the price an extra 10, 20 or 30 percent is reason enough.

"Oh, if we pre-assemble it, a larger shipping carton will be required," is one reason given. "And we cannot absorb that extra cost. We have to pass it on to the consumer."

That's us.

Naturally, if the shipping carton is larger, the truck won't hold as many cartons. Add on 10 percent.

The bigger cartons also will require more warehousing space. That's good for another 10 percent more. Or maybe even 15.

Price markups become a never-ending process. That means the unassembled set of TV trays that found its way into our house recently bearing a price tag of $39.95 would have cost a hundred bucks at least if the manufacturer had finished the job.

But noooooo, Mr. Bigshot Factory Owner and his hired hands couldn't do that. They put the four trays together and did a pretty good job of it, too.

So far, so good.

Then, as if to punish people who don't want to go to the table to eat, they gathered up 37 pieces of wood and metal, poured the smallest ones into a plastic bag and crammed the rest into the box with tables. There also was an assembly diagram and an unwritten message: "OK, Sucker, we've done all we can for a measly $39.95. Put this rack together yourself."

Everyone who has worked in a furniture factory or passed Woodworking II, please hold up your hands. Nobody. That figures.

Normally, such put-it-together-yourself projects are tackled with not even a glance at or a thought about the instructions. That usually means skinned knuckles, a naughty word or three and at least one "Why don't we just eat at the table? We don't need these #*&+@%! trays."

But some little voice from somewhere kept saying, "Read the instructions."

She was right. All those misspelled words in the list of parts were an omen. This wasn't going to be easy. No way.

Example: "Attach parts (E) and (G) to the leg spindles."

There was no blankety-blank bleep-bleep part E. Well, there was, but not what needed to be attached to the leg spindles. Part E was a little tool called an Allen wrench, which is not to be confused with a Bob wrench, a Tom, Dick or Harry wrench or even an Alan wrench.

The job took more time than anyone would want to admit. Even a minimum wage pay scale would raise the cost of these $39.95 trays to equal or more than the cost of a portable TV that could be carried to the dining room or kitchen table.

We used the trays once. When we folded them up to put away on that put-it-together-yourself rack, one busted.

That may not be good grammar, but that's what it did. It busted.

The store was more than happy to take back the set with the busted table and give us a new set.

It took every bit as long to assemble the second rack as it did the first. Probably because of that darn Alan wrench.

March, 1992

That silly rabbit let us down

Crises come and crises go. We usually survive them.

For instance, there was a major one at our house on Christmas Eve of 1953 when, as parents of a 13-month-old son, the woman I survive crises with and I discovered at 3 a.m. that battery-powered toys do not come with batteries.

The Energizer Bunny didn't come to the rescue, but a long-gone truck stop a couple of miles up the highway saved our . . .

uh, necks.

And there was the time the blizzard hit Cincinnati in 1977 or '78 and bus service to the Northern Kentucky suburbs came to a skidding halt.

Not to worry. In Northern Kentucky, the carry-outs are only a few hundred yards apart, often not that far. And even blizzards don't close the carry-outs. Stop at every second or third carry-out to get warm, in one way or another, and a Kentuckian can get home without a bus.

But those crises were kids' stuff compared with the one that descended upon our house on Jan. 1.

You know what happens Jan. 1, don't you? Of course, you do! Some of you awaken with a monster headache. Others spend the day dismantling the Christmas tree.

And still others settle down in front of the TV—remote control in one hand, beverage of choice in the other—and welcome the baby new year with a man-sized helping of college football games. Eight bowl games! Can you believe it? EIGHT!

There was only one problem: Hit the remote clicker to go from the Hall of Fame Bowl to the Cotton, the Citrus or the Blockbuster (which is a stupid name for a bowl, almost as bad as Poulan Weed Eater or whatever it's called) and nothing happens. The same two teams remain on the screen; there are six more out there on three other channels but my clicker can't find them. This was no problem, it was a crisis!

Man cannot live by bread or Hall of Fame Bowl alone. What to do, what to do?

"Maybe it's the battery," suggested the crisis sharer, trying so very hard to mask her glee. Of course, that's what's wrong, it's the battery. We'll just stick another battery in there and let the games begin. Or, at least, continue.

But this particular clicker didn't take just any old battery. It required a strange-looking battery like none other in the house. The clicker to the VCR runs on a pair of double A's; the one for the bedroom uses two triple A's. None of them is interchangeable.

Wait a minute! Where's that clicker for the TV the lightning hit a couple of years ago? It was the same kind of set this one is. It will work!

But it wouldn't. It had a dead battery, too. It takes still a different kind of battery—a 9-volt job, same as the smoke detectors. Hey, that's an idea.

"Don't you dare!" warned crisis mate, the glee fading.

But I did. And as soon as time ran out on the Miami Hurricanes and Alabama was clearly the No. 1 college football team in the land, the battery was returned to the smoke detector and the TV was turned off by getting up and walking across the room.

We had learned how to do that back in 1986 or '87 when a toddler grandchild was visiting from Kentucky.

The TV clicker disappeared for two or three days and it appeared we were destined to spend the rest of our lives getting up and walking across the room to turn the TV on and off, the volume up or down and to switch from one game (or whatever else is on TV) to another.

We finally found the clicker where any grandparent should have known to look first: in the Cheerios box.

January, 1993

It's time to switch to paper plates

This isn't the merriest of times around our house.

Oh, the Christmas tree is up all right (but that's another story!). The halls are decked and the wassail bowl would be filled with holiday cheer if we knew what a wassail bowl was and, more importantly, owned one and knew what to fill it with . . .

Just about all of the holiday preparations are completed, except perhaps shopping, addressing and mailing cards, baking, cooking and cleaning.

It should be a joyous time. But it isn't.

There was a damper on the spirit of the thanksgiving season as well. We had much to be thankful for. Our health, for starters. And our children, grandchildren and all the rest of our family. Good friends. A modest home. Good food. Just about everything a body could ask for and reasonably expect . . .

But the Thanksgiving Day menu wasn't as extensive this year as in the past. There was a turkey, of course, and dressing, mashed potatoes and gravy and a few sweet potatoes. But many of the traditional and favorite side dishes were missing for the first time in years.

It'll most likely be pretty much the same for the Christmas meal. A baked ham, some kind of potatoes and a salad, maybe another veggie. But we won't overdo it; it will be a relatively easy day for the cook.

The problem, you see, is our dishwasher.

It's broken.

It gave up the ghost right about the same time our turkey did. You fill it full of dirty dishes (which are always plentiful around our house and doubly and triply so on any holiday), put in some kind of powder to get them clean and push a lot of buttons and . . . nothing happens. The machine makes noises, the lights blink on and off as if wondrous things are taking place inside and soon the cycle is completed.

But the dishes are still dirty. They're toasty warm from the drying cycle, but still food-smeared nevertheless.

"What you need to do," numerous well-meaning friends, relatives and visitors start to say.

"What I am going to do," the woman I now dry dishes for replies, "is absolutely nothing until after the holidays. The dishwasher is old. I'm not going to wipe out my Christmas budget by paying a repairman for a service call, parts and labor. And I don't have time to go looking for a new one."

Case closed.

You know what that means, don't you? It means there isn't a whole lot of cooking going on at our house. It meant a skimpy Thanksgiving dinner and assures the same for Christmas Day. On a paper plate, maybe.

You plan a big menu, cook a big meal and one thing is as certain as holiday leftovers: You have a mountain of dirty dishes. Greasy. Dried gravy. Yukky stuff.

That's not something you want to see when the dishwasher gives them back to you looking exactly as they did when you put them in.

I swore off dish-washing in May, 1951, at Ft. George G. Meade, Md. Never again, I declared, after being rousted out of bed at 4 a.m. for my introduction to something called KP.

Dish-washing was a fun time at our house in the late '60s and early '70s. We had two daughters then and they had friends who would pitch in and help. They would wash dishes and sing. That's when we discovered one of our girls had a beautiful voice, which led her to a degree in music education at a time when schools were cutting out music to save money. She never did find a music-teaching job.

After the girls left home, it was time to buy our first dishwasher. It couldn't sing. It is time to buy another. I didn't like KP in 1951 and I like it even less now. The only difference is now I get to sleep with my commanding officer.

December, 1993

Bad things happen to good people

Before you go any farther than the first paragraph, please understand this: I am not asking for money; not one penny. Nor am I begging for your sympathy, although I won't turn my back on you if you should offer some.

The main reason for what follows is that I think you deserve a warning and I think I owe it to you to pass one along. That warning is: What has happened at our house could happen at yours. I hope it doesn't.

What happened at our house is this: Nothing works. Well, that's not completely true. A lot of things do work properly and for that we are most thankful. But several things don't work properly and it seems the list is growing with each passing day.

You may recall my telling you that our dishwasher took a leave of absence back around Thanksgiving Day. What a time for a dishwasher to go AWOL! Turkey gravy all over all of our plates, dried stuffing, caked cranberries, sweet and mashed potatoes. How can traces of everything that looks so good when you sit down at the table become so ugly when you start clearing the dishes away. And where did all those pots and pans come from!

Just a few days of washing and drying by hand—with everyone expected to pitch in and help—made it clear that this appliance must be repaired quickly. And it was . . . for about a month. Then it quit again. Age, of both the dishwasher and its users, dictates that the machine has to be replaced.

Then there is the electric range. We didn't have a clue that anything was wrong with it until two favorite cake recipes turned out to be miserable failures on Christmas Day, of all times. We blamed it on the anticipation of the arrival of children and grandchildren later in the day. The woman who bakes cakes hadn't paid sufficient attention to what she was doing, the man who eats them concluded.

But when a dish of scalloped potatoes emerged from the oven less than half done and a pizza fell far short of expectations the next day, the message was clear: this thing isn't working. It probably will have to be replaced, too.

The remote control garage-door went out weeks ago, but that's no big deal. We keep in shape by backing out the car, then pushing the switch and dashing out the door before it closes. It's something you shouldn't do in front of grandchildren.

"Don't do that Grandpa (or Grandma, depending on the culprit)," scolds a 6-year-old know-it-all. "That's dangerous; you could get killed. You'd spank us if we did that." We probably would.

Tearing a leaf off the calendar didn't help. Shortly after 1994 and all the snow arrived, the cable went out. When it returned three-plus days later, the set in the bedroom didn't perform properly. Every channel was scrambled from a few seconds to several minutes. When the picture finally came in, changing channels brought more scrambling. It wasn't a pretty sight.

But the big set downstairs was still OK. Until the middle of this week. During the evening news, the picture began shrinking. All of the anchorpeople became midgets. Maybe it'll get better if I turn it off, then back on, mused the resident electronic genius. He turned the set off; it has refused to come back on ever since.

There's more.

The vacuum cleaner doesn't. Well, it does for a few minutes, then it stops. It starts again. And stops. This goes on and on.

Which is exactly what the blower on the furnace does—go on and on. It hasn't kicked off since November.

One day this week, the head of the house reached for her eyeglasses and started to put them on. One of those things that go from your head to your ear fell off. No way can you find one of those tiny screws without your glasses.

A few hours later, we went into a restaurant for a late-night snack after a basketball game. I picked up the menu and one of the lenses popped out of the my specs. Good thing we hadn't ordered yet; it would have landed right in the middle of my biscuits and gravy.

The next morning, I picked up the phone to call one of the many, many repair people we need. The phone was out.

Are we jinxed or what? Just about everything in the house is broke. And we will be, too, by the time we get everything repaired.

February, 1994

What will they think of next?

Let's run this by one more time and make sure I understand this fantastic offer.

I know it's fantastic because the multicolored pamphlet that came in the mail with the free roll of film told me so. OK, so it didn't actually say fantastic. But it did say things such as "See your pictures on your computer," "Amaze your friends with a computer slide show," "Put photos in your letters," "Send pictures via modem." Things like that.

If that isn't fantastic, well what is it then?

This all started a few days ago when a 5 1/2x8 1/2-inch packet arrived in the mail from the company that does our film processing. We don't have a lot of film processed . . . two or three rolls at Christmas time, a few more on birthdays, anniversaries, family reunions and other semi-red-letter occasions.

We take the film out of the camera, lay it on the desk, a dresser, nightstand or whatever happens to be handy and there it stays until the next Christmas, birthday, anniversary etc. rolls around. Then we hurry and get it to the film developer so we can find out what we shot and forgot.

All that could change, however. And here's why:

"GET YOUR PICTURES ON DISK!" commands the first page of the fantastic offer. The command is in do-it-now black type against a background of colorful pictures, the most prominent of which shows four happy people frolicking at the beach in water that barely comes up to their ankles.

Now, listen: If I'm going to drive 700 miles or more to the

water deeper than my ankles. Not head high, mind you, but at least to my knees. But let's move on.

On the next page, the equally bold command is "SEE YOUR PICTURES ON YOUR COMPUTER." The background is the same four up-to-their-ankles-in-saltwater merrymakers, but something is different. It's not a photo this time; their image is now on a computer monitor.

How about that!

It's the latest in photographic technology, my film processor advises. In fact, this is something experts in the field didn't expect to see for years, the introductory letter boasts. Now I can shoot up a roll of film, let it lie around somewhere for weeks or months, then send it away and have my choice of prints, slides, a computer disk or even all three.

How about that again!

But I'm not so sure about all this yet. You see, over the years we have filled a box large enough to hold a computer monitor (and all the packing material) with photos. There also are two shoe boxes sitting atop the computer box. They, too, are filled with pictures. All kind of pictures—school pictures of children, grandchildren, nieces, nephews, in-laws, outlaws, perfect strangers and imperfect strangers. Some of them are even in focus and were snapped with the proper shutter speed and lighting. Others are . . . well, you know, the kind that so many of us take and that should have been filed in the trash can years ago.

There also is a collection of slides dating back to the late 1960s. In addition to all the special occasions cited earlier, these show school proms, high school athletic events, plays, graduations and marriages. At last count, there were 5,800 slides filed and indexed in trays. There were also about 600 (or roughly five years' worth) still in the envelopes the film processor packaged them in. They could all be blanks, for all we know.

Thank Kodak, Fuji, Polaroid etc. that we never got into home movies and video tapes. I don't think we can afford to get into computer pictures. It's not totally a dollar-and-cents thing, because the film processor assures us "It's not expensive." But all of those boxes of photos, all those trays of slides and all of those packages of slides not yet in trays take up a lot of room. So much room, in fact, that we wouldn't have had room if we had decided to get into reels of home movies and cassettes of video tapes.

Even if we had lots of room, there's a certain amount of danger in putting things on computer disks. Hit the wrong key and ZAP! whatever's on the screen goes to that Great Floppy Disk in the Sky. I know. I file stuff there all the time. That is a poor place to keep the family album.

July, 1994

8-Potpourri

You take a little of this
and a little of that and add
a little more of each and what
you get is this.

'You can have a whole pie by yourself'

Her face is a little more wrinkled than it was a few years ago. She doesn't stand quite as erectly, nor is she as sure-footed. Her vision isn't as sharp.

But that's to be expected when one approaches 80. That many years, no matter how good they have been, have taken their toll.

Of course, it wasn't only the years. There was help from rearing five children of her own, along with being a surrogate mother of sorts to 10 younger brothers and sisters.

One arrived, it seemed, every two years, often less. That meant staying home to take care of younger ones. Missing so much school often meant not getting promoted every year, but the other children would have done the same for her if their roles had been reversed, she reasoned. That's what family is all about.

She can recite the year, month and day each of the brothers and sisters was born, along with those of her two daughters and three sons and their 15 children. She may stumble a little when recalling the same vital statistics for 11 great-grandchildren.

She also can tell you almost the precise minute two of her brothers and one sister were called from this Earth.

"We've got to get a tape recorder and get that all on record," a younger sibling declared. "She knows things no one else in the family does and when she's gone, no one will know them."

Her memory is flawless. That's one thing that hasn't been damaged by the wear and tear of 80 years. It might not call up entries from bygone days as quickly as a computer, but its files are filled with details, right down to the color of a little girl's favorite dress or the year one of the kids had the measles or chicken pox.

Oh, the memories. There are many she would like to forget—a half dozen wars, the Great Depression, far too many recessions, deaths of loved ones. But for every bad memory, there were so many good ones—all those healthy children and grandchildren, for instance, and all their achievements, whether it be a gold star on a grade school paper, a job promotion or similar good fortune.

Education is one particular area in which this woman with limited education takes great pride. Missing so much school had kept her from going beyond the eighth grade, in reality quite an accomplishment for many young women in the 1920s.

Only one member of her large family became a high school graduate, so she was determined that her children do so. Not only were all graduates, they and their spouses and children since have earned 19 associate and bachelor's degrees from college, nine master's degrees and two doctorates.

Grandchildren, nieces and nephews almost are hypnotized by her stories of bygone days at family gatherings.

"Talk some more, Mamaw," a child will beg. "You make us feel like we're right there with you."

These were children who grew up in the late '60s and the '70s; she had grown up in the teens and '20s.

The young folks knew TV, malls, space shuttles and two or three fast cars in every driveway; Mamaw grew up with pie socials and cake walks, popping corn in front of an open fireplace, traveling by horseback or in a horse-drawn buggy with heated rocks wrapped in blankets to keep chilled feet warm.

She recalled tending a big garden with only a hoe or, in good times, a mule pulling a plow. When the crops were harvested, two or three thousand jars of fruits, vegetables, jellies and even meats would be canned and stored into a cellar to feed a big family during the winter.

Her audiences found it hard to believe people actually slept on feather beds, straw ticks or even corn shucks. Her offspring were from the inner-spring and water bed generation.

Mamaw could hold their attention easily with tales of all-day trips to the county fair and, if the old car was capable of such a journey, to Coney Island. Preparations always began the night before—frying chicken and making sandwiches. There rarely was money for concession stand food.

Mamaw's children always looked forward to weekends "because you never knew who would come to visit and stay overnight." That meant baking 10 or 12 pies and at least two or three cakes. The chicken population had always declined by the time Monday rolled around.

There still is plenty of pies, even in the era of grandchildren scattered all over the country. A grandson told two friends from Texas "you can go to my Grandma's house and have a whole pie by yourself." And they did.

Before the last traces of blackberry, coconut cream or raisin pie is wiped from the corners of every mouth, someone asks to hear a story. It doesn't take much coaxing.

One of their favorites took place when Mamaw was just barely into her teens and the big social event for boys and girls that age was going to the revival at the little church down the road. Mamaw couldn't wait, not because of the promises of salvation, but mainly it was a brief escape from chores and attention commanded by her brothers and sisters.

One of the sisters was just a few years younger but old enough to cry and plead to go along.

"Well, get your dress on, comb your hair and come on if that's the only thing that will shut you up," Mamaw finally gave in.

Once they reached church and sat down, Mamaw noticed her

sister, in haste, had grabbed a brand-new but homemade dress from a hanger and put it on wrong side out.

Mamaw doesn't embarrass easily, but that was one time she was. She jerked the sister to her feet, marched her outside and pulled the dress over her head. Once it was put back on properly, the two sisters returned to their pew, heads high in pride.

Memories . . . they're made for sharing.

November, 1992

Seeking for a class on how to schedule classes

"Do you know what I think I'll do?" I said to no one in particular the other morning.

"I haven't the slightest idea what you think you'll do," replied the woman who so frequently answers such questions. "But I can name several things that I'm pretty sure you will not do, such as putting in storm windows, raking leaves, washing the car, sweeping the porch and so many other things that you say you think you'll do but never get around to."

"What I think I'll do," I continued, calling on so many years of ignoring her well-practiced sarcasm, "is go down to Shawnee State and sign up for a class this fall. If I can't be a teacher anymore, maybe I can be a student."

That got her attention.

"Sign up for a class? What in the world would you take?" she wondered.

"I haven't the slightest idea," I answered, flunking the first pop quiz of the new academic year. "But I know I can find something."

"I have a fall quarter schedule, you know. Picked it up out at the fair last month. You remember, Dr. Veri was working in the Shawnee booth that afternoon. He also gave me a couple of those big plastic cups with a bear on them and a tip to a possible story.

"You know, that's the first time I ever saw a college president working in a booth at a county fair. I bet the presidents at The Ohio State University or UC or Ohio U never do anything like that."

I hope you noticed I capitalized the T on The Ohio State University; it's very important to The OSU that you do that, not only when you write it, but also when you say it.

"Of course, I don't want to take an 8 o'clock class," I explained, recalling nearly a decade of advising students as they attempted to come up with the perfect schedule. "No one ever wants an 8 o'clock class. I remember several actually changed their majors because one of the classes they absolutely had to have was offered only at 8 a.m. That's hard to believe, but it's true.

115

"A lot of kids would never take early afternoon classes because they didn't want to miss their soaps. Heck, I bet they could have missed some of those soaps for the entire quarter and not lost a thing in the story line.

"And it was tough getting girls into classes between 10 and 2 in spring quarter. They said that was the best time to catch some rays. The guys didn't want classes then either because it was prime girl-watching time."

"What's that have to do with your schedule?" she interrupted. "You said you were only going to take one class. You don't watch soaps and you're too old to be out in the sun or watch girls, anyway."

"I know, I know," I protested. "But Shawnee has a lot of evening classes and I'm not going to take anything at night. I might doze off in class and not wake up until the next morning and find myself in an 8 o'clock class. And I told you that 8 o'clock classes are out."

"What you ought to take," my ex officio academic adviser directed, "is some kind of computer class. You know good and well you've had that modem thing on your computer for nearly three years and still don't know how to use it."

"Computer class?" I wailed. "No way! Do you realize there's a 7- or 8-year-old kid studying computers at Shawnee and I hear he's acing it! He's so sharp he's writing a book on how to use computers that a child can understand. I can't take a class where a 7-year-old kid would make me look like an idiot.

"I'll just wait until his book comes out and learn from it."

September, 1992

A little of this, a little of that

Much ado about nothing. Or vice versa.

The following message, so long that the car had to pass twice before it could be read in its entirety, was crowded onto a bumper sticker seen in Kentucky:

"Live so the preacher won't have to lie at your funeral."

OK. It won't be much fun, but let's give it a try.

* * *

There wasn't quite so much commotion to take all eyes away from the bride, but it was obvious everyone wasn't paying attention to the preacher at a wedding we attended the other day.

The fellow seated on the aisle in the last pew at the back of the church leaned forward and whispered something to the person seated in front of him. It looked as if he put something into the other's hand.

Then, it was a woman, I think, who tapped the person in

116

front of her on the shoulder and did the same thing. You know, like, "Pssst, pass it on."

The scene was repeated row after row until the little game reached the mother of the bridegroom. She calmly, but very quickly, got the about-to-become-a-bride's wedding ring onto the little satin pillow where it belonged and with plenty of time to spare.

Somehow, the tiny little band had slipped off the ribbon that was supposed to hold it firmly in place as the ringbearer self-consciously began his "how-in-the-world-did-I-ever-get-roped-into-this?" trip up what looked to him to be an endless aisle.

Relatives and friends, who had spotted the ringless ringbearer as he began his journey, searched frantically before finding the wedding ring on a stairway leading from the church basement.

The aisle-seat relay team did the rest. All's well that ends well.

* * *

A crowd that eventually numbered seven or eight hundred was gathering outside the three or four entrances to the Tennessee Room of the Opryland Hotel in Nashville, Tenn.

There were women wearing long and short dresses, high and low heels and cowboy (girl?) boots. Some men wore tuxes, some wore jeans. Some wore tux jackets and jeans. There were four-in-hand ties and there were string ties.

Ten-gallon hats were commonplace, some might have even held 20 gallons without losing a drop. Every man who didn't have on boots wore regular dress shoes.

Except one.

He was attired in a handsome business suit, a nice long-sleeved shirt and a good-looking tie. He was dapper from head to ankles.

On his feet were rubber flip-flops.

"He must have something wrong with his feet," whispered a sympathetic bystander who was sitting down.

"Something wrong with his feet, my elbow!" replied her companion. "He's got something wrong with his head. He just forgot his shoes when he packed his suitcase."

January, 1992

Simple wedding, but what a reception!

Nancy and Bruce married a couple of weeks ago.

It was a simple, traditional ceremony in a little Baptist church near Nancy's home in south Alabama.

Nothing was overly fancy. She was pretty, and he was a little nervous. There were only two others in the wedding party, his father and her best girl friend.

But then came the reception. Was it ever different!

When guests made their way from the church to the Fellowship Hall, they were greeted by stuffed animals, bales of straw, straight-back kitchen chairs and benches to sit on and walls covered by four bright quilts.

The centerpiece of the bride's table was two stuffed pigs about a foot tall and all dolled up in formal wedding attire. The groom's cake was on a table marked with a small fiddle and nearby was a sketch of a team of mules.

"You should have seen their faces," Nancy's sister, Brenda, said of the well-wishers. "People were looking like this," she added, her head moving quickly from side to side and her eyes resembling two big circles.

No more than six or seven knew ahead of time what was behind the doors of the Fellowship Hall. For the other 175, it was a complete surprise.

" 'Oh, this is so cute' was the typical reaction," another of the ringleaders said. "Whose idea was this?"

Mainly it was that of the bride's sister and a close friend. They enlisted the help of a couple of others. Nancy was in on it, of course.

"It started out as a joke," said one of them, a self-described distant relative but a close friend.

"Someone said 'Let's have a real country reception'," she continued, "and Nancy said 'That's a good idea.' And it just evolved."

What it evolved into was things such as servers attired in blue-jean skirts, white blouses and red neckerchiefs. Instead of punch from fancy crystal, they used a tin dipper to serve lemonade from a galvanized bucket.

The dip for veggies was in a ceramic chicken, cheese straws were shaped by a pig cookie cutter and there were 332 tasty (you guessed it) pigs in a blanket to munch on.

A big, round wash tub was filled with iced Cokes and beside it was a basket of moon pies.

"Everyone thought the moon pies were just decorations and didn't want to eat them," one of the reception planners said. "But I saw some of the men putting them in their pockets."

It's just a coincidence, they said, that the bridegroom is a farmer in the northeastern part of the state. They say they didn't even think of that when they started preparations about four weeks before the wedding.

Nancy was pleased with how her guests reacted.

"Everyone felt more relaxed," she believes. "Some people said it was 'the most fun wedding I've ever been to.' "

There was only one thing out of place as Nancy and Bruce put a picnic basket filled with cake, a bottle of champagne and other goodies into the back of a Nissan 300ZX and headed for the mountains of Gatlinburg, Tenn., and horse farms of Lexington, Ky.

They should have been traveling in a pickup truck. Or a horse-drawn buggy.

September, 1988

Terrible Tony and the pink flamingo caper

You may have missed this story a short time ago. You know how it is. On a busy news day, sometimes an important story falls between the cracks and either is ignored entirely or at best fails to get the attention it deserves.

This was one of them.

It's about an ever-vigilant, on-the-ball sheriff's deputy down in Florida who arrested a 3-year-old for uprooting a neighbor's pink flamingo lawn ornaments.

It seems that a little tyke by the name of Tony, described by the Associated Press as "a wide-eyed boy with curly blond hair," wandered onto his neighbor's lawn, pulled two ornamental plastic flamingos out of the ground and dropped them on the driveway.

The neighbor did what any red-blooded, law-and-order American would do. He (or maybe it was a she) called the police.

The deputy sped to the scene (the AP didn't say whether blue lights were flashing and sirens wailing), pondered the evidence and then filed an affidavit charging Terrible Tony with criminal mischief. 'Way to go, deputy! Tony, his parents and perhaps all of society will thank you for your heroic action someday.

Never mind that your superior officer immediately stopped the charges. Forget that the captain said, "It was poor judgment. Obviously, we don't condone this."

Don't worry because he said both you and the sergeant who reviewed the affidavit may face disciplinary action. You were simply doing your job, the best way you know how. The captain is just a softy, one of those bleeding-heart do-gooders. He's probably even a card-carrying member of the American Civil Liberties Union, perish the thought!

See, you know and Tony's neighbor knows and just about everyone but that dumb captain knows that if you let Tony get away with felling flamingos . . . well, who knows what he'd try next?

You let a kid pull up flamingos today and tomorrow he'll sneak into your yard and pluck your petunias.

After that, it's downhill all the way. He'll turn off your sprinkler. And maybe progress to running back and forth through the cooling spray. Perhaps with no clothes on!

119

Oh, you did the right thing, Mr. Deputy. You and the complaining neighbor did what was necessary to keep Tony—innocent wide eyes, curly blond hair and all—on the right path . . . not the one leading to someone else's pink plastic flamingos.

If he had been allowed to get away with this caper, next thing you know we would have been reading about Tony traipsing over to Walt Disney World and pulling Mickey's tail or plucking Donald Duck's tail feathers.

But rest easy, Mickey, Donald and pink flamingos everywhere. The crime-fighting deputy is on the job, ticket book and pen (or maybe it's a red crayon) in hand. Tony has learned his lesson. He has promised not to upend any more flamingos.

"That's a no-no," he was quoted by the Associated Press, which also reported he was rolling in a pile of laundry on his living room floor.

But can we trust him? And is there any kind of law against rolling in a pile of laundry on the living room floor? Call the deputy and check it out.

P.S.: Some people think the kid deserves a medal for upending the pink flamingos. Their only criticism is that he just left them lying in the driveway instead of putting them into the garbage can. Some people!

June, 1990

All that money, but where's Ed?

Whew! The first week of 1992 has been extremely hectic around our house.

Not only are we still trying to get the Christmas tree down (we never rush this task), the trimmings put away and all the tiny, sparkly lights off every tree and shrub in sight, we're also making preparations for two big celebrations: the 500th anniversary of Chris Columbus's journey to Columbus, Ohio, and the 200th anniversary of Kentucky statehood. Credit for that probably goes to someone like Colonel Sanders, Rick Pitino or maybe even Cawood Ledford.

But, shoot, that's not all. We've been looking at new cars. Big, expensive ones. And learning to spell condominium, as in Florida.

You see, we fully expect to come into a pile of money very, very soon. Lots of bills. With big numbers on them. And pictures of people I don't know on them.

The first hints of this impending wealth began arriving a couple of weeks ago, courtesy of Uncle Sam's Postal Service. It tries to deliver as much of this kind of mail as possible in late December, apparently in hopes of easing the pain of that bundle of IRS and Ohio tax stuff that is a harbinger of the new year.

Most of our riches probably will come from Reader's Digest. Documents from at least three of its sweepstakes have been filling our mailbox regularly.

One of them is for $5 million, another, I think, is a $10 million package and I can't remember what the other is. But what the heck, what's a million dollars when you're talking about many millions?

The woman I balance the budget (sometimes) with frequently complains because she has to mail so much stuff back to Carolyn Davis and the others who sign all that sweepstakes mail. Good gosh, woman, what's a 29-cent stamp compared with five or 10 billion! I'll buy her a whole book of stamps as soon as Ms. Davis sends me the cash.

One of them even promised to have an armored car deliver our winnings. But that's a bit much. Just make a direct deposit, like Social Security and Troy State University does. We haven't seen any real money for so long we might not know what to do with it.

There are also the Publishers Clearing House, which has $10 million burning a hole in its treasury, and Magazine Marketplace. It wants to give us a million, which is hardly worth fooling with when you consider what the others want us to have.

The only disappointment in all this is the absence this year of anything from Ed McMahon. We always used to get letters from Ed with his beaming face telling us we may already have won bundles of bucks.

But not this year. At first, we thought it might be because Ed and Johnny are going to be out of work in the spring and he's going to have to start watching his money. But the people next door got THREE letters from Ed. And only two people live there.

There's one other troubling thought, too.

Reader's Digest does a marvelous job of condensing books and pages-long stories into a more readable length.

Wonder how small it would shrink a $10-million jackpot?

January, 1992

One man's junk, another's treasure

"Hey, I know something you ought to write about," a friend called out at the flea market the other day. "Junk mail."

Yeah, that's not a bad idea. Heaven (and our postman) knows we get a handful of it almost every day.

So we dug out one of our county fair shopping bags and began saving our so-called junk mail. Decisions, decisions.

What goes into the junk mail sack? Is it something that is

unwanted? If that's the criterion, then everything that comes from the electric, gas, water, sewer, garbage collection and cable companies qualifies. So do those twice-a-year tax bills and auto tag renewal reminders. And a lot of other stuff.

But that can't be treated as junk. To do so could get us in a heap of trouble. Perhaps it's the second-class mail we all get so much of.

Nope. Can't call that junk. Our second-class deliveries include USA TODAY, which is read from top to bottom, front to back five days a week. And two other out-of-town daily newspapers, a weekly and a college newspaper.

Junk? Get your hands off my newspapers before I break your fingers.

So what's in the junk mail sack at the end of 30 days? Let's take a look.

* Four sales papers from each of four different department stores, one from a biggie in Cincinnati and Dayton whose closest store is in Huntington, W.Va., and one from a local furniture store which should have been delivered to the folks next door.

* Ads, complete with coupons, from three pizza restaurants, one steakhouse and one chicken frier.

* Unbelievable offers from two storm window dealers, a carpet cleaner, a hairdresser and an auto service.

* Catalogs from an auto parts and accessories store, a computer company and a gift shoppe. There also was one from a place called "After the Stork." At our age? Get real.

* A book club offering "four books, four dollars, no strings."

* Letters advising that an American Express and two VISA cards were reserved in our name and that a local bank would lend us a minimum of $1,500 at 13.5 percent interest for up to 36 months.

* Another telephone company volunteering to be our long-distance carrier.

* Four missing children cards asking "Have you seen me?" and carrying sales pitches for four different companies on the other side.

* Two insurance proposals, one on our car, the other on our lives.

* And three fat little envelopes with these messages in varying sizes of type and colors on the outside: The Most Valuable Book Ever Published; How To Beat the IRS; DIRTY SECRETS—What the airlines, hospitals, doctors, car dealers, banks, etc. don't want you to know.

How much of it is junk, how much goes in File 13?

We always look at the sales circulars; someone may have a real bargain. And the food coupons aren't junk when your stomach is growling.

Toss the credit card offers. They were addressed to the head of the house, while only the loan offer had my name on it. There's a message of some kind in that and I don't especially care for it.

The three fat little envelopes also made a speedy exit. We've had a rule around our house for about 35 years after we learned a piece of mail we tossed out contained a crisp $1 bill: Never throw ANYTHING away without opening it.

The three fat little envelopes were an exception to that rule. Their messages couldn't have been clearer even if they had said, DIRTY SECRET—This is junk.

Then a story in the paper the other day settled the question for us. It told of a Californian who became a millionaire in the direct-mail business and now is planning a museum that will be a shrine to junk mail.

He's proof that one man's junk mail is another man's treasure.

September, 1990

In search of a plain, brown wrapper

Whatever happened to those plain, brown wrappers that allowed delivery of something you might consider to be a little embarrassing?

You used to see or hear of them a lot.

I remember them back in the early 1940s when I worked after school and Saturdays at a grocery store and meat market. Sanitary napkins, and probably a lot of other feminine hygiene products I wasn't even aware of, were packaged in plain, brown wrappers.

Not any more. They and a lot of other things that once were under the counter now are in bright, eye-catching packages displayed prominently for all the world to see.

Same goes for magazines and other publications we might want to read—or look at the pictures—but didn't want the neighbors to see us buying or sticking out of the mailbox.

Many of the publishers promised delivery in a plain, brown wrapper. Plain, brown wrappers are passe now. We just let it all hang out.

A couple of plain brown wrappers would have been appreciated at our house recently. Once was when we reached into the mailbox and pulled out a yellow envelope with half-inch tall black, capital letters: HERPES TEST RESULTS. At the bottom, with a black line under and over the length of the envelope, in smaller letters: PERSONAL AND CONFIDENTIAL.

I would certainly hope so.

At least that envelope was only 4x7 1/2 inches long. Only

the postal carrier and every mail handler between here and Athens, Ga., saw it. Not to mention any computers and electronic scanners and other electronic technology the Postal Service employs.

The next one was the size of a small billboard and had to be folded to get it into the mailbox. I suspect that many of you received this mailing, too. The return address was that of Beer Drinkers of America, which has National Administrative Headquarters in California somewhere.

Come on, guys, give me a break!

It's bad enough that my letter carrier and all of the Postal Service between here and Atlanta think I've been tested for herpes, now they probably picture me as a two-fisted beer guzzler who probably is too soused to tear open the envelope to find out the results.

I can explain the herpes letter. It came from a former student of mine in Alabama who observed, "Hope the dirty envelope didn't get you in trouble with the neighbors or mailman up there in conservative Ohio."

The Beer Drinkers of America apparently didn't care what the neighbors or mailman thought. All that organization wanted was for me—"and thousands of people across the country"—to complete an opinion poll opposing an increase in the federal excise tax on beer and possibly contribute $5 to Beer Drinkers of America. It would forward results of the poll to Senators John Glenn and Howard Metzenbaum and U.S. Rep. Bob McEwen. It would keep the $5, of course.

I did neither, which is my way of getting even for sullying what's left of my reputation.

It isn't necessary to attempt to get even with the former student. I did that several years ago, every time I gave him a grade.

If ever anything cried out for a plain, brown wrapper, it was his grades.

March, 1991

Really, I don't want the right opportunity

OK. This was someone's idea of a practical joke, right?

Someone—I hope it wasn't you—saw one of those coupons in a newspaper or magazine and decided to fill it out. Only instead of your name and address, you used mine. Correct so far?

Then a short time later, our poor, overworked postal carrier had another piece of junk mail to crowd into our mailbox, along with three daily newspapers, a weekly, Service Merchandise sales fliers, various and sundry envelopes that go into the waste basket unopened and an endless flow of bills.

But never any letters. That's why we call them postal carriers nowadays, never letter carriers. They rarely carry letters anymore. People don't write letters, so there aren't any to carry.

Think about it. When was the last time you got an honest to goodness letter to open?

That's one of the reasons this particular piece of junk mail caught my eye. That and the fact that on the outside of the black envelope in 3/8-inch yellow letters was the bold declaration: **You have everything it takes to make it except for one thing.**

That'll get your attention in a hurry. I kind of had reached the point where I sort of thought that I had everything it takes to make it. Whatever it was I was trying to make.

So what's missing?

You never saw an envelope opened so quickly, unless it was an income tax refund.

"Dear Mr. Joseph:

"With the right opportunity, nothing can hold you back.

"Because you've already got most (underlined) of what it takes to make it: A DESIRE—deep down in your gut—to do more than just get by; PRIDE—in yourself and your abilities; and SMARTS—the common sense to make your own (underlined) decisions. (I really liked that (underlined) part!)

"But what you don't have is the opportunity (underlined; I never saw a letter with so much underlining) to use those abilities to the fullest. That's why you shouldn't miss this chance to find out more about Marine Corps opportunities (underlined, of course) like these."

Aaargh!! Marine Corps!?! Talk about your sneak attacks. This was a search and destroy mission carried out to perfection.

The letter went on for another page and a half, but it just wasn't the same after that. Even the underlining lost much of its punch.

It listed outstanding benefits ("Name one other job that gives you FREE room and board, FREE dental and medical care, 30 days' paid vacation—plus travel and adventure"); job training in 36 career fields; education benefits to help you go far (yeah, I've read about some going as far as Panama just in the last couple of months) and good pay that goes a lot farther (see Panama).

Hey, I've got nothing against the Marines. One of my best friends is a member of the tough team. The few. The proud. The Marines.

In fact, he could have been the practical joker who supplied my name. No, he wouldn't do such a thing. He'd do it to me, perhaps, but he'd never do it to the Marines.

Those Marine dress blues are about as sharp looking as military uniforms get. And that trim on the top of their hats that Marine lore says was to keep them from pouring boiling oil (or something) on their own mates always made a fascinating story.

125

But let's face it, I'm not what the Marines are looking for.

The letter continues: "To be a Marine is to say, 'I can go the whole nine yards! I have what it takes to be the best, part of the elite team.' "

I can't go the whole nine yards anymore. Even nine feet may be a little much. Unless I can sit down and rest. I've seen those recruiting posters. The U.S. Marines want you. They probably wouldn't have wanted me 40 years ago. They darn sure wouldn't today.

But it was (underlined) a nice letter.

January, 1990

You know what makes me mad? WHACK!

A favorite speech teacher at Northern Kentucky University a few years back had a little exercise he used to get students to put some punch into classroom talks.

He had them bring a pet peeve and an armful of newspapers to class and roll them—the newspapers, not the peeves—tightly to about the thickness of a baseball bat. Then they would wrap several rubber bands around the rolled-up newspapers to hold them together. The paper bat was to be used when the speaker wanted to emphasize something he or she was saying.

"What makes me really mad," the student would begin, "is when I get a busy signal (WHACK!) on the telephone (WHACK!). About the second (WHACK!) or third (WHACK!) time I get so angry (WHACK!) I could throw the (WHACK!) thing out the window (WHACK! WHACK! WHACK!)!"

You'd be surprised how much noise rolled-up newspapers can make when applied firmly to the top of a desk . . . or to an unsuspecting classmate sitting nearby. And how much confidence it can give an "I'm not very good at this" public speaker. Some of them seemed to walk out an inch or two taller after delivering a WHACK!ing good speech.

So, with a few copies of the newspaper rolled tightly, here are a few gripes to take a few WHACK!s at.

What makes me really mad is:

Litter.

Drivers who run traffic lights and stop signs as if they weren't even there.

Drivers who don't signal that they are going to make a right turn before they get to where you sit and wait, afraid to proceed because they've tricked you into thinking they're going on through the intersection. Then when they do turn right, you've waited so long that traffic won't let you go now.

Drivers who do signal turns, but don't look to see if the signal cancels after the turn. You follow the blinking things for

126

miles, wondering when or if the car us ever going to turn. A comedian (perhaps Gallagher, although the spelling may be wrong) once did a bit about such drivers. He said they continue on, blissful in their ignorance, while the turn signals blink the continuous message, "I'mafool, I'mafool, I'mafool."

WHACK!

Six-month-old magazines in the doctor's office.

Anything (especially me) in the dentist's office.

WHACK!

Adult fans who boo high school athletes.

People who raise umbrellas at football games. Not only do they block your vision, they also dump their rain in your lap.

People who, you know, say you know every, you know, three or four words in a, you know, sentence. You know what I'm saying?

WHACK! WHACK!

My clothes smelling like someone else's smoke.

TV weatherpeople interrupting with an advisory right at the very best part of the show. When was the last time one broke in during a commercial?

TV shows continued next week.

The sound increasing a couple of decibels during commercials.

Misspellings in the newspaper.

Bad grammar by the talking heads on the tube.

People who say or write verbal when the correct word is oral. Everything written or spoken is verbal . . . unless it's in sign language.

Columnists who scold, lecture, nitpick and preach. WHACK! WHACK! WHACK!ety WHACK!

October, 1989

Fine for littering . . . just try it

Do you ever pay much attention to road signs as you're cruising along the highway?

I don't mean the signs that say "McDonald's (or the burger of your choice), next exit, turn left." What I'm talking about are the official-type signs, the ones intended to give you the information that will make your journey safer, quicker, more enjoyable.

Most of us pay attention to the ones telling us the speed limits in the particular area we're passing through. We may not brake to 40 when we enter a 35-mph zone. And we stay in the lower 60s even when we know we're not supposed to exceed 55 unless we're driving on an interstate outside a congested, metropolitan area.

Somewhere someone told us once that we can get away with

127

driving 62 in a 55-mph zone or even 72 when the signs clearly say the max is 65. They'll give you a 7-mile cushion, our all-knowing friends say, referring to the officers who keep tabs on such things.

For some reason, I doubt that. It would be my luck, I remind myself, when the speedometer begins to creep higher and higher, to run into a state trooper or a local gendarme who got up on the wrong side of the bed, had a run-in with his wife at breakfast or was scolded by his sergeant shortly before he climbed into the cruiser.

"Where's the fire?" he would ask, following up with a request for my driver's license and registration. A few minutes later, he would drive away and leave me sitting there clutching a ticket that wouldn't get me into anything except the local court.

We were traveling in another state—I think it was Texas—a few years ago and entered a small town where the "Welcome to What'sitsname" sign added this warning:

"Speed limit 55 miles per hour—not 56, not 57 but 55. Strictly Enforced."

I may be dumb, but I'm not stupid. Believing every word that sign said, I slowed, not to 57 or 56 or even 55; I backed off to 50 and gave myself a 5-mile cushion. There's no way of telling what kind of problems the local Smoky had encountered earlier in the day.

But that's not the kind of road sign I'm talking about, either.

I mean signs that pass along such information as "Bridges freeze before roadway."

OK. I'll buy that. Maybe there's room on that pole to put another sign advising, "Consumption of alcoholic beverages impairs your ability to drive a car, operate machinery and may cause health problems." Or "Surgeon general's warning: Smoking causes lung cancer, heart disease, emphysema and may complicate pregnancy."

The last two are just as factual as the first and a lot more frightening. And that's the point, isn't it, to scare us into being careful?

Some signs are just a tad confusing. "Park and pool," for instance. Are we being invited to stop for a swim or to shoot a game of eight ball? Never mind. My skinny legs and slight paunch look awful in trunks, and I don't carry a cue stick in the car.

"Deer crossing" is another puzzler. You never see a big buck or any of his family using the crossing. They always dart out in front of you about 100 yards before or after you get to the sign.

One sign is personally offensive to a large segment of the male population. I'm referring to the one that warns us about "Soft shoulders." Some even go so far as to say "Narrow and soft shoulders."

Hey, we can't (or won't) all pump iron or shoot up with steroids to look like the second coming of Michael Jordan, Wayne Gretzky, Ken Griffey Jr. or Troy Aikman. It's the narrow, soft-shouldered guys like us who make the Adonises look so good. If the highway people can't come up with better wording, those signs should go. Immediately.

"Falling rock" and "Fallen rock" are confusing. Are we to watch out for rocks that are falling or already have fallen? About the time we look up for one that's falling, we'll smash our car into one that has fallen and is lying there in the highway.

"Watch for ice on bridges" is another sign you see frequently, no matter what the time of year. While I was teaching in Alabama a few years ago, a student swore he sat along the highway for three hours one August afternoon and never saw as much as a single ice cube.

Don't believe every sign you read. "Fine for littering," for example. Yeah, sure. Fine and dandy. Just try it. You get caught and you'll pay for it. Maybe even spend a few nights in the slammer.

August, 1994

Junk to you, memories to me

"It's about time," the woman in charge said in her most authoritarian tone of voice, "that you go through these cards and throw most of them away. There are two boxes of them," she continued. "Where in the world did they all come from?"

"These cards" that she was condemning to the wastebasket were those little 2x3 1/2-inch business cards people hand you when they want to impress you. And the two boxes they were in were only the size of a business card and six inches long. I mean, we're not talking crates or cartons or even shoe boxes. Getting rid of them isn't going to give us that much more room in the house.

Besides, I told her in my most unauthoritarian tone, I can get rid of one box quickly. They're my old cards and I haven't had any business since the summer of '88.

I no longer have an employer or a job title, plus the address and phone numbers are wrong. Other than that, they still look kind of impressive, don't you think? She didn't answer. But I don't need 750 of them—I think that's how many that box held. What do you say if I keep eight or 10 for souvenirs and toss the rest of them? But I'm going to keep that nice little box. It might be useful sometime.

"Keep a few of your old cards if you want to," she answered. "But I don't see any sense in keeping the rest of them."

She's right, I said to myself as I began sorting through them.

Most of these are from former students. Lord only knows how many times they've changed jobs since they gave me these cards.

Whoa! Not so fast. These are all doctors' cards. I can't throw them away. We may never get a health care program through Congress, so I'm hanging on to these. Would you believe six of them? I hope they never all send bills at the same time.

And here are a couple of keepers. They're funny, both from the same fellow. One has his name, address, phone number and affiliation on one side. On the other side it says: "This is a FREE TICKET. It's not good for anything, it's just free!"

The other card has the man's name and "No phone, no address, no money, no worries, no business, no prospects." Under his name, the card has this message: "Retired and lazy. When I get the urge to work, I just lie down until the urge passes."

I wonder where all of these former students are now. They all had good jobs when they gave me these cards. They should be doing even better by now. I'm not so sure about these two, however. Both were working in public relations for state governments, one in Alabama, the other in Georgia. Both administrations since have changed, so they're probably somewhere else now.

I know this one has a new job. The card says she was an information specialist for the Alabama Peanut Producers Association in Dothan. The last I heard, her job title was Mamma and she was living in Memphis.

By far, most of these cards are from newspaper people. But there are also three from photographers, two artists and three crafts people. There also are cards from a disk jockey, a gospel singing group and a good ol' boys (and girls) bar in Alabama. "Lester's Flat is where it's at. Fine Bluegrass and country music. Home of the Frito pie." What a great place to spend Saturday nights! But it's closed now.

Oh, my, I can't throw this handful away. These are my kids' cards, along with a few of my own from Cincinnati newspaper days.

The children's cards pretty much tell the stories of their careers from the day they left college. Two of them went into journalism, the other is a teacher. She had cards. I can't find any of hers and don't recall what they said. Probably something like "Miss Joseph, school marm, sit down and be quiet."

I can't throw these away. None of them. Too many good memories. Let's throw something else away and make room for these. It's just a small box.

September, 1994

Birds and bugs and X-rated stuff

Let's talk a little about nature. What I want to talk about specifically are some on nature's littlest creatures: hummingbirds, june bugs and lightning bugs.

I started to retype (or recomputer or whatever you say since typewriters became almost extinct) june with a capital j, but I did something that very few reporters, myself included, do nowadays. I looked it up in the dictionary and guess what? It's not supposed to be capitalized. How about that? You learn something new every day.

But it's a little bit of learning I'll rarely use because I hardly ever write june bugs. I also hardly ever see any, either.

All right, I know this is July. But I never saw any in June, nor did I see any in May. How come? What happened to them?

To tell the truth, and I try to once in a while, the last time I saw any june bugs was six summers ago in Woodland Cemetery in Ironton, Ohio. I just happened to be in Ironton for some reason and decided to drive through Woodland, one of the prettiest burial grounds around.

The june bugs were everywhere. They were thicker than fleas. Much more attractive, too. There were so many june bugs that the noise they make when flying sounded like a swarm of bees. Several swarms, actually.

They also made a crunching noise when my car passed over them on the ground. Hey, I blew the horn but they didn't get out of the way. Probably didn't hear it because of the bee-like noise.

It had been years since I could remember seeing any june bugs, and I haven't seen any since.

There were lots of june bugs when I was a kid. Or at least that's how I remember it. They were probably bigger then, and flew faster, too.

But that didn't keep us from catching them and tying a length of thread to a leg and holding the end of the thread while the june bug flew in circles. We were entertained easily then. I just don't seem to see june bugs anymore. Something else I haven't seen much of this summer are hummingbirds. Wonder if you could catch a hummingbird, tie a string to its leg and hold it while it flew in circles. Start, stop, hover. Over and over again. But I digress.

I know there are hummingbirds out there. People tell me they are as thick as june bugs used to be. Some folks say they have so many hummingbirds that the little darters have to take a number before helping themselves to the feeder or poking their sharp little noses into the bloom of a flower.

Not at our house, however. We keep our feeder filled with fresh sugar water. There are and have been flowers of all kinds blooming for a couple of months. But there's not a hummingbird to be seen. I wouldn't really tie a string to one's leg like a tether ball. Honest. That brings us to lightning bugs. We have lots of them. Literally millions. Maybe; I haven't actually counted them.

We sit on the front porch and watch them blink at us, like so many amber signal lights on tiny little cars. I know kids still catch them, because I've seen my grandchildren chasing them and putting them into a jar. I can remember little girls catching them and encircling their fingers with the lightning part of the bug to make a glowing ring. They made a pretty ring, but they sure did stink.

Lightning bugs aren't so innocent as you think, flying about going blink, blink, blink without sound. That rhythmic flash is part of a signal system that brings the sexes together. How about that! We've been sitting on the front porch and watching an R-rated show. Maybe even X.

July, 1995

9-High fashion

Clothes make the man,
someone once said. That's
right. They often make him
quite uncomfortable, not
to mention sometimes
making him look downright
silly.

My ties' statement: We're terribly out of date

The occasion was a luncheon meeting in Ironton, about 20 miles up the Ohio River from where I live . . . I call it a luncheon only because it started at 11:30. Otherwise, it was a full-fledged dinner. Fried chicken and everything else that anyone possibly could want to eat.

The bad part was that this was a gathering of senior citizens. There were about 70 present and you probably could have counted on the fingers of one hand the number of people whose doctors would have smiled and said, "Go ahead. Eat all the fried chicken and anything else you want."

It was that kind of meal even before it was time to visit the dessert table. Calories, cholesterol . . . all the things that keep doctors, druggists and hospitals working overtime. But that's the way things are at these kinds of gatherings.

I was to be the speaker.

"I think I'll wear my new Christmas sweater," I declared to the woman who accompanies me to these feeding frenzies and does a remarkable job of overeating in her own right.

The sweater I was speaking of is one that only a wife (or, in this case, a daughter who is very much like her mother) would buy for a man in the autumn of his years. It's a cotton, crew-neck assembly of two-inch vertical stripes in bright blue, burgundy, white, deep purple and green, not always in the same order. The big stripes are separated by smaller irregular-shaped navy stripes.

Do I like it? Yes, very much.

Would I have bought it for myself? Good heavens no!

I'm old and becoming more conservative with each birthday. I lean to browns and dark blues, although I sometimes get reckless and put on something in a pastel. I even have one sweater that is pink! But I don't wear it often.

Neither do I wear the new Christmas sweater often. It's the kind that when you wear it once, people who see it won't soon forget it. Wear it more than two or three times a year and they'll think you have it on everyday.

But I didn't get to wear it to Ironton that day.

"I think you should wear a coat and tie," answered the woman who already had visions of cherry cheese cake, pecan and every other kind of pie imaginable and other almost obscene desserts dancing before her eyes. "After all, you are going to a church and you are the speaker."

So I wore a coat and tie, along with a shirt, trousers and everything else that decency requires. My tie was so out of style I should have been ashamed. For one thing, it's not nearly as wide as is the fashion these days. For another, it was a small pattern in contrast to the colorful fashion statement the ties of the '90s make. The only statement my ties make is that they're almost as old as I am.

I do have two ties that are very much up to date both in width and design. One is navy and covered with a small forest of fully decorated Christmas trees. The other includes all of the colors my new sweater has, and a few more to boot. Its design includes, jack o'lanterns, ghosts, witches, graveyards and other spooky things.

Neither tie would have been overly appropriate at this time of year. The ties, by the way, were gifts from the same daughter who bought the sweater. That figures.

"This will be a sweater crowd," I predicted as I knotted my tie. "I bet the preacher and I will be the only men there with coats and ties on."

There were, indeed, only two men in the room with coats and ties on. But the preacher wasn't one of them. One was me, of course. The other was a dapper-looking 90-year-old. I'll tell you, we sure looked nice! Even if our ties were narrow and not the least bit '90ish looking.

March, 1995

OK, who stole my pants pockets?

The time has come, and probably passed, to make a fashion statement. It won't necessarily be a stylish fashion statement. After all, by the time most people, women excepted, reach my age, we're too slow to keep up with the fashions.

In fact, it doesn't even have to be a fashion statement. It might be better presented as a question:

WHO IN THE SAM HILL DESIGNS THIS STUFF WE'RE EXPECTED TO WEAR?!

Which prompts another question: Who is Sam Hill?

And yet another and another: Why is he doing this to us? Why must we wear some of these stupid things?

For example:

I recently was given a new pair of shorts. I don't know what the occasion was. Father's Day is still weeks away and my birthday is even farther. (Or should it be further? Oh, never mind.)

I don't know what kind of shorts they are. But I do know what kind they aren't; they aren't underwear shorts. They might be called walking shorts, because I wear them when I walk to the fridge or to the bathroom.

They could even be called running shorts, except that wouldn't be truthful because I never run and these shorts won't either as long as I'm wearing them.

But the name isn't the problem. The problem is pockets, or

135

lack of same. Most of my pants have at least four pockets, two in front and two in the rear. There are even a few pairs of jeans around that have five pockets—one supposedly to carry a watch in. When was the last time you saw anyone carrying a watch in one of those watch pockets? How old was he?

But for some dumb reason dictated by fashion designers, when they cut off the pants legs and make shorts, they also eliminate one or more pockets.

How come?

If men carry enough to fill four pockets when they wear long pants, what do they leave home when they wear shorts?

Someone, please tell me, because I'm afraid I may be leaving the wrong things. The same goes for sweat suits. Or warm-up suits. Or whatever name you prefer.

Personally, I'd prefer not to sweat. And anything I have to warm up for will leave me too tired to do it after I finish warming up. And how many pockets do most warm-up-to-sweat suits have? None, according to a survey of the ones hanging in my closet.

Where are you supposed to carry your car keys and driver's license? Or a few bucks to buy a towel for mopping up all that sweat.

You could get a fanny pack, suggested the woman who buys my shorts and sweat suits.

No way, I replied. You may call it a fanny pack, but most men my age would call it a purse. And only men who design clothes with too few or no pockets would ever think of carrying a purse.

That's my fashion statement for today.

Maybe some day we can get around to another statement about leisure suits.

May, 1993

Shelby knot joins hangman's noose

A recent trip out of town to attend a wedding meant it was time to put on a tie. No big deal. Just reach into the drawer, get one, then another and another and another until you finally find one that wins approval of the woman I go to weddings with. Wrap it around your neck and away we go.

If it were only that simple!

First of all, you're not supposed to reach into a drawer for a tie. Drawers are where you keep underwear and handkerchiefs. Ties belong on racks. But I don't have any up yet. After all, we've only lived in this house six months. You can't get everything done overnight.

It isn't easy finding the right tie when you have to root

through a drawer. By actual count, there were 59 to choose from.

That's not bragging. Why would anyone brag about a collection of 59 pieces of cloth four to five feet long and tied in a knot that is distant kin of a hangman's noose?

They're just something you have to have when they're part of your daily uniform, something you wear eight to 10 hours a day and the second thing you shed when you get home at night, just seconds after you kick off your shoes.

My tie rack, if I had one, would hold all kinds and colors—knits, wool and silk, solids, stripes and a paisley or two, basic blues and browns but also a few reds, pinks and yellows. There also are a few school ties, along with a couple that aren't likely ever to see the light of day again. One is a scene of the Delta Queen steamboat tied up at Cincinnati; the other is covered with pig's rumps and the obvious implication that the wearer is a male chauvinist pig. Not true.

Those two, along with maybe four or five others, are the long out-of-style wide jobs—four inches across and looking more like a bib than a tie.

Remember the ones we wore about 25 years ago? About an inch or an inch and a half wide and more like a shoe string than a tie. Ties of the last few years have been a very happy medium—about two inches wide—but there are rumblings in fashion circles that those coverall types may be coming back. Oh, well, I still have my fountain and pigs to fall back on.

You see, I don't have to wear ties very often anymore. A wedding once in a while. Or a funeral. And maybe to impress somebody . . . or cover a spot on my shirt.

The wedding was only the fifth time I've had to choke myself in the last six months. Prior to that, I had put one on every day—except Saturday—since 1953 when I was turned loose by the Army and returned to my civilian occupation. You get to the point you can even tie one while still about two thirds asleep—if you really don't care what the knot looks like and if the thin end is sometimes longer than the wide.

Do I miss them? Yeah, I suppose so. About like I miss going to the dentist, working nights at the newspaper factory and grading papers at school.

Not wearing ties also means I don't have to worry about learning how to tie the new (?) Shelby knot. Perhaps you've read about it in the newspapers or in magazines. And maybe you have seen a diagram of how to tie it.

You do everything backward from how you learned to tie one on as a youngster. But when you're finished, the right side is out as it should be, the short end is still backward but no one can see it anyway. Some say the Shelby is the perfect knot, precisely balanced, absolutely symmetrical and exactly proportional.

The Shelby is named for a TV guy in Minneapolis who learned it from a 92-year-old man who said he had been using it for 30 years.

The Neckwear Association of America says the Shelby is indeed something new. The association checked it out and couldn't find any similar directions for such a knot in "Getting Knotted—188 knots for Necks," everything you ever wanted to know about knots for ties, scarves, ascots and cravats distributed by a silk mill in Italy.

You read it right—188 knots! No way.

Since Shelby got all of his publicity, another man has come up with a booklet he says he got from a Milwaukee clothing store in the 1950s. It calls the same knot a reverse half-Windsor. Whatever.

Personally, a nice clip-on would be just fine with me . . . if there wasn't the ever-present risk of it falling into your dinner plate. Ties collect enough gravy stains without that happening.

October, 1989

If the shoe fits, put an ad on it

The subject today is marketing, one which I know absolutely nothing about. But that has never stopped me before, so let's get to it.

To be a little more specific, the subject is the marketing of shoes and newspapers. But not in alphabetical order.

I recently acquired a new pair of athletic shoes. They are white, they fit well and are very comfortable. That's about all I ever look for in a pair of shoes. Except price. That's the first thing I look for anymore.

The price was right on this pair of shoes. Still, I wouldn't have bought them if the decision had been mine.

The reason I wouldn't have bought them is that every time I put them on I become a walking billboard for this particular brand of shoes. When I buy something and pay my money for it, I don't think I should walk around wearing an advertisement for that particular brand of shoes.

I feel that way about the car I drive, but there's nothing I can do about it. Oh, I suppose I could get a bucket of paint and a brush and go over every place the car's name appears. I guess leaving it alone and advertising the car free is the lesser of two evils.

But back to the shoes.

I have three pairs of athletic shoes that still look decent enough to wear out in public. One pair has the brand name in one place: right under my heel. I put them on, lace them up and nobody knows what I'm wearing. And, I might add, I strongly suspect that nobody cares!

The second pair has the maker's name in three places: in the heel where it's covered by my foot, on the tongue where it's hidden by the laces and in little, tiny letters on the left side where it can be seen only by dachshunds and short poodles.

But the new pair of shoes? Six places, plus a big red initial nearly an inch high on the tongue. I'm not kidding; I am really serious about this.

The shoemaker's name is in raised letters on the rubber heel, on the right front, on the tongue just under the big, red initial, in the sole under my heel and on the bottom of the sole where it leaves an imprint every time I take a step . . .

The sixth place, in letters three quarters of an inch high, is on the back of the heel. That's six times—count them again if you don't believe me—on each foot.

If I need anything written in big letters on the backs of my shoes, believe me, it would be LEFT and RIGHT.

The other area in which I am troubled by nagging questions is the marketing of newspapers. This never happens at home. When I'm home, I merely walk outside—or run when it's as cold as it has been lately—and reach into the plastic tube and get my newspaper.

But it's a different story when I'm out of town. First, I have to find a vending machine that has the current day's paper inside. That isn't always the case and it's a lesson I have learned the hard way. Then I have to find the right combination of coins in my pocket. That rarely occurs.

Last weekend, I ventured out of town and was seeking a morning newspaper in below-zero temperature. Most newspapers cost 50 cents, so I found two quarters, double parked and walked confidently—in my shoes with the name on each six times—to the newspaper box.

But the sign on the front of the box said "Daily 35 cents." Good deal. Shivering, I found a dime, deposited it and one of the quarters and tugged on the front of the box. It wouldn't open.

I slammed the heel of my freezing right hand against the coin return and the machine spit out my dime and my quarter. After repeating this twice more, I finally saw a second sign that said "Saturday 50 cents."

I deposited two quarters and got my newspaper. What I didn't get was an answer to this question. How did that big, old dumb-looking newspaper vending machine know that this was Saturday morning? How did it know that it was no longer Friday? What would it have done if I put my quarter and dime into it on Sunday?

If it's so darn smart, I'll invite it over to read all the free advertising on my new shoes!

February, 1996

139

10-Season-ing

Everyone talks about
the weather . . . and some of
them make a bundle of bucks
doing it. In the meantime,
we're digging our way out of
6 to 8 inches of partly cloudy.

A severe case of cabin fever

What do you do when there is 30-plus inches of snow on the ground, the temperature has been as low as 34 degrees below zero and the thermometer still refuses to climb more than a few degrees above the big 0? You're too old to have to get out and go to work and too smart (or perhaps the word is lazy) to want to venture out of doors?

I repeat: What do you do?

Nothing.

Absolutely nothing.

You can't do anything. Not even if you wanted to. Those numbers above are together in a conspiracy to keep you from doing anything.

And don't question those numbers, either. That's what we have been told in the papers and on radio and television (until the cable went out a couple of days ago). If those numbers are deep enough and cold enough for the news people working out there, this couch potato isn't going to challenge them.

Day 1 wasn't so bad. You pull a couple of chairs over in front of the picture window and marvel, "Isn't that beautiful!"

That's followed by "It's still coming down" (as if it ever went any other direction), and finally, "Damn, isn't it ever going to quit?"

Beauty still is mentioned every now and then, but not nearly as often as it was shortly after daybreak. You've long since abandoned the picture window view. You occasionally walk to the kitchen to see if the snow is as deep in the backyard as it is in the front. Or upstairs where the view is pretty much the same except you see the snowflakes a few feet farther off the ground.

And you count your blessings. You've got a roof over your head, plenty to eat, the house is warm and you're alive, which is a lot more than can be said for some of those people in California who were awakened by an earthquake instead of an alarm clock.

Day 2 would be a rerun if it hadn't stopped snowing. Besides, there is something else to think and even worry about: The TV weather guys (and women) are using all their best adjectives to describe how cold it's going to get. Look for a record (for the date) low of as much as 18 degrees below zero, they warned.

Wow! It's a good thing we decided not to use the fireplace. We need to save our wood in case the electricity goes off.

Day 3. The thermometer on the back porch shows a reading of 30 below. Hah, hah, it never did work right. About that time, the man on the radio bellows, "It's 34 degrees below zero in Wheelersburg!" As I said, the thermometer on the back porch never did work right.

Can't turn on the TV to watch the Weather Channel or see how the earthquake victims are doing; the cable is off. The radio is lecturing: Don't go out unless it's an emergency. Highways are hazardous. Don't use the phone unless it's absolutely necessary; leave the lines free for emergency calls. Don't call any of the emergency numbers unless it's an emergency. Don't use any more electricity than you absolutely have to. Turn the thermostat as low as you can and still be comfortable. Don't use your washer; don't use your dryer; don't use the dishwasher; don't curl your hair.

Hey, we're already saving electricity. The TV hasn't been on since the cable went out. Thank goodness for all those books we never found time to read. Plus, the newspaper was delivered today (three at once) and the mailman ran, bringing two copies of USA TODAY (which, because mail delivery is a day late, really are USA Yesterday).

Day 4. The weatherman was right again. He had predicted above-zero temperatures and 1 to 3 inches more of snow, which hardly would be noticeable on top of the 30 inches that have been out there for what seems like years.

Cable is still off. Perhaps we should deduct two days the next time we pay the bill. After all, we're still billed when we're away from home and don't use it.

I'm tired of reading. It's too soon to write Christmas thank-you notes; we can't be sure everything fits or works. I can't put the outside lights into storage because they're still on the trees or under three feet of snow.

What do you mean it's snowing again? Are you sure it isn't just blowing off the trees? You're right, there are no trees out in the street. It has to be more snow. Aaaarrrrggghhh!

January, 1994

Weathering the storms

"Everybody talks about the weather, but nobody does anything about it."
—Editorial, The Hartford Courant, Aug. 24, 1897

And do they ever talk about the weather. On and on and on. Never before have so many said so much about the weather. And told us so little.

"A high pressure area over the Lower Ohio Valley will hook up with a stationary front that has just been lying around doing nothing and the result will be a bunch of squiggly lines starting in the Upper Plains and extending through the smiley faces clustered over the Eastern Seaboard. And that's the weather picture today. Back to you, Sally."

OK. So that's the weather picture. But what the heck does it mean? What's a high pressure area? What do all those squiggly lines mean?

Can't someone just tell us if it's going to rain tomorrow? Is it going to be hot? Or should we take sweaters or jackets along when we go out? Don't give us that humiture stuff. It's not even in the dictionary.

Forget about heat indexes and wind-chill factors. When the temperature gets so high or so low, that's all we need to know. Giving it another name and adding or subtracting a handful of degrees isn't going to make things any better . . . or worse.

Remember the old days when the newscaster would tell you all you needed to know about the weather in two or three sentences and the newspaper could handle it five or six lines in one of the ears at the top of Page One.

Not any more.

TV gives us three to five minutes every noon, 6 and 11 p.m. The morning shows seldom let 30 minutes pass without a briefing. Willard Scott has become rich and famous. All this because of the weather . . . whether the forecasts are right or not.

Some stations have weather staffs as large or larger than their sports departments. Come on, guys (and gals)! Let's get things back into perspective. Just let someone walk over to the window, take a gander at the skies and then tell us what's happening.

Newspapers are equally guilty. USA TODAY discovered weather as a marketable news commodity. Soon, just about every newspaper in the country was splashing color over half to three quarters of a page telling us everything we never wanted to know about atmospheric conditions, dew points (that's another one that is never explained), jet streams, Arctic Clippers, Siberian Expresses and Mr. Scott's toupee.

Want to know how hot it was yesterday in Manila? Of course you don't. But it's there, along with high and low temperatures and some other unexplained abbreviation for 30 or 40 foreign cities.

The big bonus is a box telling "How to use this page," including a scale for converting temperatures from Fahrenheit to Celsius. That comes in handy when you're sweating out 90-degree temperature and the scale reminds you that it's only 32 degrees Celsius.

The always cheerful TV boys and girls rarely tell us what they're talking about. It's highly confidential, to be shared only by members of the AMS, whatever that is.

Most of us watch every day at suppertime and again at bedtime for the temperatures around the area, the national weather map, the latest satellite picture and live radar. These include lots of arrows, big blue H's, big blue L's, big red H's and L's, and on one channel, yellow H's and L's. Maybe they all mean the same thing. Who knows? They're accompanied by drawings of puffy clouds, lighting bolts and raindrops so big that if one ever hit you, you'd be a goner for sure.

Then comes the moment we've all waited for: Tony's (or Joe's or Toni's) Forecast. Not our forecast or the station's forecast; it's Tony's or whoever's. Keep that in mind the next time it's so far off target you're driven to naughty words.

Of course, living where we do, all of this doesn't mean much. Our weather reports come from Cincinnati and Columbus, Ohio, and Huntington and Charleston, W.Va . . . If what they predict happens to hit around the Portsmouth area, fine. If not, so be it.

Forget the 24-hour Weather Channel. No one could possibly want to know THAT much about the weather.

If you don't like the weather in the Ohio Valley, just wait a few hours; it'll change. Anyone who has lived here just a few hours knows that.

August, 1990

Rain brings flood of bad news

It seemed so unreal.

For three or four days, we had watched television footage of flooding in south Alabama. Our ears perked up when CNN or the Weather Channel mentioned "Elba, Alabama."

Of course, by the time we got into the next room and in front of the TV, the story had moved on to another water-soaked location and we had missed the news from the little town scarcely 30 miles from where we had spent six years in Dixie.

The next day, we heard that six people had lost their lives when a van plunged into a rain-swollen stream, the occupants unaware that a bridge had been washed out. The reporter didn't even mention the location, apparently feeling what had happened was more news than where it had happened.

The next report told us where: Florala, Ala., the pretty, sleepy little stateline town, its streets lined with palm trees, that we had driven through countless times while going to and from Florida beaches.

Memory could dredge up only two other times Florala had been in the news: Once when a bicycle rider—or maybe it was a runner; memory does tricks after a few years—had plunged into a water hole to cool off and lost a leg to an alligator, later when the town's 80ish mayor became the center of much controversy because of antics that caused him to become known as the "voodoo mayor."

But we had never seen anything like we were seeing now, from 700-plus miles away.

It all became painfully real when our local newspaper carried a 4-column headline, "Ten dead as rivers swell in Alabama," followed by "3,700 left homeless after non-stop rain." Both figures went higher on succeeding days.

The wire service dateline was Elba, Ala.

This was unreal.

The rivers mentioned in the Associated Press report—the Pea, the Choctawhatchie, the Alabama—all had appeared so harmless during our acquaintance. The worst thing about the Choctawhatchie was trying to spell it. The Pea was remembered most for warnings about the poisonous cotton-mouths that would sometimes drop from overhanging trees almost into the laps of unsuspecting boaters.

But flooding? You got to be kidding.

No one was kidding. Unless it was Mother Nature. And even then, it was a poor joke. We remembered Elba as the little town—also on the route to the beach—that was the home of several good friends . . . the little town where we went for the wedding of a former student.

But last week there had been 16 inches of rain in two days and an earthen levee had given away.

Now, our newspaper told us, 1,500 of Elba's 4,400 residents were homeless, floodwaters still lapped at downtown rooftops and damage and cleanup costs were expected to be in the millions of dollars. And those snakes no longer were in overhanging trees; they were swimming all over town.

A short distance away, in Dale County, the newspaper said some 500 people had been forced to leave their homes in and around Newton.

Newton? Why, that's where we went a couple of years ago to a going-away dinner for a fellow faculty member. Of course it is. We can't even remember seeing any kind of stream with the potential for such flooding.

It was real. Very real.

And if we didn't have newspaper and television reports to confirm it, we have no farther to look than our own Ohio River and no longer ago than the '40s and '50s to remember that what is happening in Alabama now happened here just about every spring.

A floodwall and a series of new dams along the Ohio River have reduced flooding in recent years, except in unprotected low-lying areas. It's been years—maybe as far back as 1937—since we've seen anything like south Alabama is experiencing now.

And for that we are grateful. The water is receding now, and it's not likely TV or our newspapers will tell us much about the cleanup. They won't have to, for what has been happening in

Alabama once was so commonplace in the Ohio Valley. The folks down there will pull together and make it an even better place to live, just as we have had to do so many times.

March, 1990

Time to enjoy summer daze

It's finally here.

I'm talking about summer, as most of you probably guessed.

Don't bother looking at the calendar and saying something like, "It's not summer yet, you crazy, old coot! Summer doesn't arrive until June 21."

I know that. That's calendar summer. That's for record-keeping purposes. The calendar starts summer on June 21 this year and ends it on Sept. 23.

That's OK. But you know and I know and all of God's creatures know that summer really begins on Memorial Day and ends on Labor Day. Really.

Summer used to begin on Decoration Day. That's what we used to call it back in the days when it came only on May 30. Then someone came up with a bright idea.

"Let's change it to Memorial Day and move it to the last Monday in May," that bright someone said. "We can close the post offices and banks and give all of the government workers the day off. We'll have a three-day weekend and jam up highway traffic for miles."

So that's what happened.

Many—not all, but certainly a lot—who used to observe Decoration Day by going to the cemetery now hop into the car and head for the beach, a lake, a park or some other exotic destination. If there is no time left for decorating graves, at least the deceased will be remembered, which is what the name Memorial Day intends us to do.

But there's more to Memorial Day.

It's the unofficial start of summer, remember? It's time to fire up the grill and cook out. Some may have rushed the season and burned a few dogs and burgers already, but that was just practice. Cookout season officially begins on Decor—I mean Memorial Day weekend.

I don't really like to cook out. I like to eat out, if there aren't too many flies, bugs, ants and other pests. But I'd just as soon let someone else do the cooking.

Bad things happen every time I attempt to cook out. I try to watch TV or read the paper at the same time and burn whatever it is I'm supposed to be cooking. Hot grease splatters on my pale, bare legs. Or on the front of my clean shirt. The charcoal goes out. Or burning grease flares up and scares everybody, including

146

me. My wife yells at me.

Why do men who never, ever think of going into the kitchen and cooking a steak or a hamburger think it's their duty to do it if it's cooked outdoors? I don't think it's my duty. If there had been any such thing as prenuptial agreements back in 1951, that is the first thing that would have been written into mine.

"Party of the Second Part (also known as Husband) will not be expected to cook steaks, hamburgers or other foodstuffs over a hot fire outdoors and in return Party of the First (and foremost) Part (also known as Wife) will be excused from such duties as chopping wood, cutting Christmas trees and changing tires."

Such a covenant perhaps would have saved a few marriages. It certainly would have prevented a lot of burned food, blistered legs and fingers, dirty shirts and spousal yelling.

Another start-of-summer ritual that is worthy of mention today is the first sunburn of the season.

But that will have to wait until another day. The tops of my legs—right where they hit the edge of my chair—are extremely pink, almost red, to be exact. And are they ever tender! I can't sit here another minute. I had no idea I was out in the sun that long the other day.

May, 1994

Help me! I'm falling

It's that time of year again.

Summer's over, or it will be in a few days.

You look at the calendar one day and it's still August. Summer. Baseball. Cookouts. A dip in the neighbor's pool. Another picnic.

Suddenly, the calendar tells you it's September. Fall. Storm windows. Leaves to rake. Homework. Time to put away the grill.

Oh, sure, officially it's still summer until Sept. 22, but we know better. That's just a line someone's been feeding us for too many years.

Fall begins when September arrives and Labor Day makes it official. Keep your eyes open and your ears alert; you'll be seeing Christmas merchandise in the stores before this month's over and carols won't be far behind.

Some people love fall. I'm not one of them, but the woman I share the changing of the seasons with is.

"I love the fall of the year," she gushes. "It's my favorite time of the year. The leaves are so beautiful" and she goes on and on and on.

Why do you always say "fall of the year"? I ask her. It's redundant. Why don't you simply say "fall." Besides, I just don't like fall.

I should. I have a birthday in the fall, this month, actually. That means I'll be another year older. Getting older isn't bad, in fact it's the wise thing to do. But one of these days, the birthdays will quit coming and you know what that means.

Everything seems to get older in the fall. Some die. Tomato vines already are turning brown. Flowers that were so pretty all summer are starting to look a little shabby; soon they'll be gone. Leaves that already are messing up the yard are just a warning of what is to come.

Fall, you can have it.

If you want to get ecstatic over a particular season, make mine spring. That's when tiny sprigs of green begin to peep out of the ground. Never mind that they'll grow into dandelions, crabgrass and other obnoxious things. At least, it's a start.

The whole, wide, wonderful world is waking up. It's a time of resurrection and life. That's why God put Easter in the spring and Halloween in the fall.

Look no further than your dictionary to find out how little respect fall gets . . . or deserves. The one on my desk devotes 87 lines to fall, most of which defines the word as a verb.

As a time of year, however, fall gets only this: Often capital F. Autumn. That's it. Spring, at least, earns an explanation of the equinoxes and a notation that it's when "the weather becomes warmer and the plants revive."

As a noun, fall's wordiest definition is: Any of several pendant articles of dress, especially: a. A kind of veil hung from a woman's hat and down her back. b. An ornamental cascade of lace or trimming attached to a dress, usually at the collar. c. A woman's hairpiece with long, free-hanging hair.

There's also this definition for fall:

A loss of virtue or moral innocence; a yielding to sin.

No wonder I don't like fall.

September, 1992

Another September, another birthday

This is not a particularly favorite time of the year. At least for one person.

This is the time of year that brings:

1. Birthdays.
2. Fall.

Just about everybody likes birthdays. Let's face it, you can't live without them, no two ways about it. For that reason, here's one loud and strong vote that birthdays continue for many years to come.

Funny thing about birthdays is that when you're young you

148

can hardly wait from one until the next. Your parents are even worse during that first year; it's as if you don't really have an age until you finally are 1. Then they count the days while waiting for you to leave the terrible (!) 2's.

Then the milestones come so quickly they're hard to keep up with. Finally, you're 5 and it's off to kindergarten. A year later, 6, and first grade.

The years go by and before you know it you hit double digits—10! And immediately you set your sights on becoming (drum roll, please) a teen-ager! Hey, this is what life is all about—pretty soon, the first date, the first kiss. (At least that's the way it was many years ago.)

The next big birthday was 16. There was something to look forward to at that age, but it's hard to remember what it was. Oh, yeah, it's all starting to come back—that's when you were old enough to get a driver's license.

Then came 18 and it was one of those good news, bad news things. The good news was that, if you had a hankering to, you could buy your first legal brew. The bad news, for the guys, was that we had to register for the draft. All that has changed, of course; the legal age to lift one now is 21 and a draft is what you might order.

You can vote now at 18, although few do. We had to wait until 21.

Birthdays start losing their glamour at 21. You start noticing gray—or missing—hair at 30. Some people consider 40 to be a midlife crisis and one person, who shall remain nameless, thought life ended at 50. He went into a blue funk that lasted until just a month or so before he turned 51.

He had another one not too long ago. Never mind which one. Just call it plenty-9 and leave it at that.

Birthdays and fall have a lot in common. Just about everyone likes fall. Many people love it. And why not? It is a beautiful time of the year. Leaves soon will be turning colors that are unmatched any other time of the year. People who live in larger cities soon will be heading to the boonies to oooh! and ahhhh! just like on the Fourth of July.

The sunsets are gorgeous in the fall. It's almost as if they reflect the turning leaves. But at least one person doesn't share that enthusiasm for the season.

For all of fall's beauty, he considers it a melancholy time. He considers it to be a time when all that we have loved and nurtured all year long is now withering, and finally dying.

Soon all of that turning foliage will be gone and the countryside will be stark and barren. Nothing is prettier than the hills of Southern Ohio and Northern Kentucky in the spring and summer, even fall. Nothing is more dismal than those same hills in the winter.

There ought to be some solution for those among us who aren't overly fond of birthdays that seem to get closer every year and who don't feel like turning cartwheels when fall arrives.

Perhaps after the age of plenty-9, birthdays could come only every 18 months or two years. But still count only a year, of course.

And fall could be reduced from three months to three weeks. No, what the heck, make it a whole month. Winter can start a week before Christmas and end the day after New Year's.

The rest of the year could be spring, beautiful, blooming spring and summer. There's at least one guy who would really go for that kind of deal if there's any way to work it out.

September, 1989

11-Life with father

In Dad's time, love
was food, clothing and
a home, not words.

Dad got a kick out of his short life

It was early spring—or late winter, if you prefer—of 1946. But the memory is still as clear as if it had been only last March. Or maybe even yesterday.

The weather was still chilly late in the evening and in the morning. Black smoke curled from the coal stoves that kept most homes warm and cozy in those days. Not too many people had gas furnaces back then, and not many who did lived on the upper end of Glenwood Avenue in the steel mill town of New Boston, Ohio.

We thought we were doing pretty well, though. We lived in one of the old mill houses—a duplex that had been turned into a single-family dwelling by cutting a new doorway here, sealing another there and getting rid of one of the two kitchens.

The crowning touch, of course, was installing a bathroom indoors! Dad seemed nearly always to work afternoon turn, punching out at 10:45 at the steel mill's West Avenue gate and getting home at 11—give or take a few minutes, depending on how fast he walked or whether anyone offered him a ride.

He'd eat a bite, look at the paper and then turn in around midnight. The last chore of the day was banking the fire—putting in a large chunk or two of coal so there would still be heat in the morning.

That meant the first one up about 6:30 the next morning had to shake down the dead ashes, put in some fresh coal and get the fire blazing.

That was my job.

It should have been a simple task. There was a handle that fit onto the grate and you gave it a few twists of the wrist and, if everything went well, the fire soon roared to life, the house got warm, Dad still was snoozing soundly and all was right with the world.

There was only one problem: me. The job didn't require a lot of skill, and I didn't have a lot. In fact, if there was any possible way to mess up, I'd find it.

Just as often as not, everything in the living room became covered with dust from the falling ashes and the house would be filled with smoke. And the noise I was making would awaken Dad.

Maybe he had a bad shift at the mill the night before. Or it could have been something he had read in the paper that upset him. But more than likely he simply was tired of being jarred from a sound sleep by the clanking of the grate, only to be nearly overcome by smoke.

Clad only in his long underwear and using some words I hadn't even heard before, he came charging through the dust and smoke and unloaded a punt that would have made any kicking coach proud. I know, because I was the football.

He had forgotten one thing, however. He was barefoot.

There was no follow-through on that punt. As soon as it landed, Dad howled in pain, grabbed his aching right foot and hopped back toward his bedroom. The last thing I saw was the trap-door on his long johns flapping on every hop, as if applauding his good kick.

Perhaps that's not the kind of story usually told on Father's Day. But it will have to do. Dad was . . . well, just Dad. He had a lot of friends at the mill, but otherwise he was just a regular Joe. All he did was work everyday—when the mill wasn't down because of lack of orders or on strike. He never took a vacation in his life, paid his bills and supported his family. He loved baseball and a cold bottle of home-brew hit the spot now and then.

He never had much, because he didn't believe in buying anything unless he could pay for it. In full. For that reason, he drove a succession of clunkers that promised adventure every time he turned the crank or ignition key.

Dad has been gone 34 years. I only knew him for a few months longer than 27, but I can't feel cheated. My brothers and sisters, all younger than I, didn't get to know him that long.

I can't remember ever telling my Dad I loved him; I doubt if either of my brothers ever did, either. And I can't remember him ever saying that he loved me. That just wasn't his style. Most men of his time were like that.

But things have changed now. Men today say "I love you" without feeling like some kind of a sissy. And they can cry without getting kicked out of the old boys club.

I wish Dad were still here today. I'd have something to tell him.

June, 1992

First and 10, do it again!

My Dad, a dyed-in-the-wool sports fan until the day he died, spent his short time on this Earth a few years too early. Or, as we prefer to think, he left it too soon.

Oh, how he would have loved to have been around in the '90s so he could have enjoyed the unbeatable combination of college football, cable television and remote control!

Truth is, baseball was always No. 1 in his book. But baseball isn't even in the same league with football when it comes to TV. He quit watching the tube back in the '50s. Everything he watched was in black and white then. That was before cable, of course, which meant his choice of channels was limited to 3, 8 and 13 and 8 was pretty fuzzy much of the time.

His only remote control was whichever of my three younger brothers happened to be closest to the set when Dad decided he wanted to watch something else.

The channel rarely was changed if a ball game was on. He was a Cleveland Browns fan because of Paul and because it was the only team in Ohio. He also liked the Chicago Cardinals because they hadn't yet moved to St. Louis and Phoenix and also because the late, great Red Grange was one of the broadcasters.

Besides, they were the only teams we could get.

Compare that slim pro schedule with the collegiate menu he would have drooled over last Saturday: Kentucky at Indiana on ESPN and Mississippi State at Tennessee on Ted Turner's Super Station in Atlanta at 12:30.

Michigan State at Notre Dame on NBC at 1:30. Houston at Illinois on ABC at 2:30. Auburn at Texas on ESPN at 7:30. Brigham Young at Penn State on ABC at 8.

Whewww! Even a few catnaps during dull spots wouldn't have kept The Old Man from sleeping good after that many quarters of football.

And heaven help the three boys if they became a little too rowdy (translation: a lamp was knocked over or an end table upset during an unscheduled wrestling match) or any one of them got in front of the screen during a key play.

Dad didn't ask any questions. He'd grab all three and set their butts afire. Never mind that one may have just entered the room and was totally innocent. He probably had it coming for some earlier misdeed that had gone undetected. Or would earn it before the game was over.

The first thing Dad would have done in preparation for yesterday's games was to send the set to a repairman to see if there was anything wrong with it. Were the Browns and Bengals really that bad last Sunday or was the trouble in our set?

Then, with remote control in hand, he would have settled in. It wouldn't have taken him long to learn that if the quarterbacks get their rhythm in sync, he would be able to switch from one channel to another without missing a play.

Kentucky-Indiana wouldn't have held his interest long; they're basketball schools, regardless of what kind of uniforms the players had on. He'd opt for Mississippi State and Tennessee and their brand of smash-mouth football.

As the afternoon wore on, the clicking of the remote control, the repetition of instant replay and the carryings-on of three brothers would have become a little much.

Dad would see—or think he saw—the Notre Dame quarterback complete a pass to a Texas wide receiver; Indiana playing a man-to-man defense against Kentucky's fast break; a Tennessee burner sprinting for a touchdown followed by an instant replay for 12 points, and, finally, a Penn State linebacker

154

throwing Red Grange for a four-yard loss.

But he would survive. And be ready for Sunday's pro games and another round with the three boys.

September, 1991

Rollin' a smoke in the days B.C.

"Well, there's something I haven't seen for a long time," commented the woman with whom I've seen things for a long time.

Oh? What's that? I asked, climbing into the car in the drugstore parking lot. "That man in the car next to us," she indicated with a nod of her head. "He got a package of Bugler out of his pocket, rolled a cigarette and lit up."

Well, I'll be darn. I didn't know they still made Bugler.

But they do indeed. And it's still in that same two-tone blue package showing what surely must be a World War I era doughboy blowing reveille on a bugle.

Memories came tumbling back as we backed out of the parking space, the corner of my eye catching the smoker taking a deep drag off his roll-your-own and the cloud of blue smoke floating lazily from his car window.

Those memories, of course were from 'way back in the mid-'40s B.C. Before Cancer, that is.

That soldier on today's Bugler package no doubt is blowing taps.

Bugler shared shelf space in those long-ago days with such tobaccos as Kite and it seems like there was one called Ripple. Or was that a cheap wine? Others were Bull Durham and a couple that served double duty as pipe tobacco as well as for cigarettes, Granger and Prince Albert.

Good old Prince Albert! Rare was the kid—well, at least boys—who never called the corner grocery store and, stifling giggles, asked, "Do you have Prince Albert in the can?"

An answer in the affirmative triggered a smarty-pants "Well, you better let him out!" and a roar of laughter from everyone crowded around the telephone.

OK, so it's not funny in 1991. But we didn't have all the television comedians to copy in those days.

Rolling a cigarette was much easier said than done. Three hands would have made the task much easier.

First, you had to get the paper in one hand and use the other to pour the tobacco out of the pack onto the paper. Then, carefully balancing the paper so all the tobacco didn't fall into your lap, you had to close the package and put it into your pocket, throw it on the table or floor or do something so both hands would be free to finish the rolling job and licking the glue-

155

edged paper that held your cigarette together. All this before you were hit with a nicotine fit.

It was a little easier with Bull Durham. That brand came in a little cloth bag with draw strings. That enabled the roller to pour the tobacco onto the paper, nonchalantly use his (or her?) teeth to pull the draw string and go on from there.

No way could you get the tobacco distributed evenly the entire length of the paper. As soon as you rolled it as tightly as you could, licked the paper to seal it and set the tobacco afire, the nearest wise guy would pop off, "What're you smokin', a Camel? I could tell from the humps."

My old man usually puffed humpy cigarettes. One day he brought home a roller that turned out cigarettes that were so round, so firm, so fully packed—just like the tailor-mades that used that very description in its advertising.

Being the oldest in the family brought with it the privilege of rolling Dad's smokes. It also presented the opportunity to slip one or two into a pocket for a few puffs later in the outdoor john.

For the longest time, I was convinced all my younger sisters and brothers were squealers. Instead, the tattletale was smoke escaping over the door or through cracks and knotholes in the outhouse.

Long before warnings were printed on packages, smoking could be hazardous to your health. Particularly when you got caught.

December, 1991

An early switch or a caning later?

Michael Fay and I have never met. Probably never will. Come to think of it, I doubt that I have ever been in his hometown of Kettering, Ohio, although I did visit some relatives a few months ago in a couple of Dayton's less affluent suburbs. He most likely has never been in my hometown.

To tell the truth, I had never even heard of the young man until he ran afoul of some very strict laws in Singapore.

But it takes only a slight stretch of the imagination to find that Fay and I have something in common. More about that later.

Michael Fay's run-in with Singapore-style justice cut loose a much greater flow of ink from the world's printing presses than blood from his caned rear end a few days ago.

For the past two months—ever since Fay was sentenced to six lashes with a soaked rattan cane, four months in prison and a fine of a little more than $2,200—there have been almost daily reports of his divorced parents' outraged reaction, what his lawyer had to say, protests by this group or that and even a plea for leniency from the President of the United States. Singapore didn't back down under such pressure, although it did reduce the number of lashes to four.

Perhaps it was encouraged by polls in this country that more often than not showed most of us felt Fay deserved what he had coming and by golly maybe that's what we need to do take back our streets from the murderers, rapists, robbers, thugs, druggies and other scum that is keeping us behind locked doors, whether it be daylight or dark.

OK. Maybe I can force myself to agree with those who protest that six—or four—lashes inflicted by an expert in the martial arts is somewhat severe for acts of vandalism that included spray-painting and throwing bricks at high-priced automobiles and possession of stolen signs and Singapore flags.

The same offenses here probably would have resulted in a suspended sentence, probation or at the most a few hours of often meaningless community service.

But Fay got in trouble in Singapore, not here. He had to answer to Singapore authorities, not ours. He lost the home-field advantage when he left Ohio and went to Singapore. Not even the President of the United States could change that.

And that's the way it should be.

Of course, it's easy to say that when you're not the one whose pasty, white butt is being torn open by a cane four feet long and a half inch thick.

Still, now that the punishment is over and Fay is healing, there are signs that he may become a rich, even though scarred, young man. There is talk of books, movies, TV appearances. Photos of Fay's bleeding buttocks are said to be worth at least a half million dollars.

We're talking big bucks, folks.

And that leads me to recall my first punishment that surely must have originated in Singapore. I was much younger than Fay; he's 18, I was only about 5. Fay is accused of using spray paint. I used matches; spray paint probably hadn't been invented.

We lived on the edge of town, in a brick house close to where Little League fields are now located. They were part of a farm that my grandfather owned then.

It was about this time of the year and the coal-burning stove had been taken out of the living room and was sitting on the back porch out of the way. Newspapers had been stuffed inside it to keep any remaining soot and ashes from being blown about.

My Dad and I were the only ones at home. He was sitting on the front porch reading the newspaper, perhaps dozing. I was on the back porch, playing with matches.

Shouts from a neighbor perhaps 50 to 75 yards away alerted Dad to the fact that flames were reaching toward the porch roof from the heating stove. The same shouts alerted me to the fact I better hightail it.

Dad was a young man then and he could move. He quickly doused the flames without any damage, then took out after me. He stopped only long enough to break a switch off a plum tree before discovering my hiding place.

I have no idea how many lashes he gave me. Who can count when you're screaming and dancing? All I know it was a lot more than four. Plum switches may not be as bad as a rattan cane, but they're rough. They're kind of gnarly, almost like thorns. I'm squirming now, just thinking about it.

It makes me wonder: Would a plum switch at age 5 kept Michael Fay from his encounter with a rattan cane at 18? Might have. It worked for me.

May, 1994

12-To your health!

As the years pass,

one thing becomes painfully

obvious: Growing old is

the hardest thing you'll

ever have to do on

this Earth.

No ifs, ands or butts about it

Sponsors of the Great American Smokeout will be happy, I know, to hear that I did not light up the other day when they asked smokers to give up cigarettes for 24 hours.

They will be even happier, I suspect, to hear that I did not light up the day before Great American Smokeout day, nor the day after, either. Furthermore, I have no intentions to light up any time in the foreseeable future.

I bet that will make them really happy!

To tell the truth (and that's what I'm supposed to do, isn't it? At least once in awhile), the last time I flicked my Bic (or whatever it was), set a cigarette afire, took a deep drag and then exhaled was on Dec. 28, 1967. It was a Thursday, I believe, about 7:30 or 8 p.m. A Kent, with a micronite filter. At least, that's what the ads and TV commercials said at the time.

You don't forget quickly the last time you did something that you had been doing since you were in your teens.

I have no idea how many cigarettes I smoked—or let burn in an ash tray—between the first one and the last. It probably was no more than a half pack, if that many, in the beginning. You can't light up very often when you're spending most of the day in school. And it's really hazardous to your health if your Mom or Dad catch you sneaking a puff at that age.

By the time I had my last one, I was into my fourth pack at the end of each day. For you nonsmokers, there are 20 cigarettes in a pack (or there used to be), so you can figure out the rest. I lit up as soon as the alarm clock went off. I reached for a cigarette if I woke up during the night, and that happens frequently when there are three babies in the house. (They didn't awaken me, but the woman who got up to see about them frequently did.)

I would have been a prime target for the Great American Smokeout had I not given up smoking nearly 10 years before the Smokeout became a national thing.

Actually, I didn't give up smoking. Instead, smoking was taken away from me. Physically. Really.

I went into a hospital in Covington, Ky., just a few days before Christmas. My attending physician took a few days off, so another doctor looked in on me.

"Is he still allowed to have cigarettes?" asked the woman who was my daily visitor. She was seated in the doorway, almost in the hall, really, because I was in isolation.

The doctor was shocked.

"You can't have those," he scolded as he took the package from my bathrobe pocket and pried my fingers from around an unlighted L&M I was trying to hide until he left.

"There's another package in his locker," tattled the woman

160

seated in the hall. He took those as well. Thinking back now, I'm quite certain he did not have a search warrant.

I had my last cigarette a few days later when I was able to sweet-talk a young reporter who came to visit me.

The Great American Smokeout probably is a pretty good thing. There are statistics and more statistics on how many give up smoking on the third Thursday in November.

Perhaps the idea can be extended to other vices as well.

We could have a Great American Drinkout and ask people to leave the lids on their bottles for he day.

A Great American Snackout might be nice. Or a Great American Gossipout and a Great American Litterout. Isn't this just great!

Hey, how about a Great American Shootout? No, that would never work. We have too many of those every day of the week as it is.

November, 1994

Medical advice: Don't read studies

NEWS ITEM: *The accepted wisdom that everyone should get a cholesterol check to try to lower their cholesterol is no longer quite so clear.*

Great! That's terrific news.

Let's see, for breakfast tomorrow, I'd like a half dozen strips of bacon, two eggs over easy—be sure the yolks aren't too runny but don't get them too done—and toast. Lots of toast and don't be too stingy with the butter.

The review—the largest ever done—has called for a scaling back of widespread national cholesterol programs.

I love it! I love it! I love it!

A cheeseburger will be fine for lunch. Make it a double cheeseburger with extra cheese. A big order of fries, and how about a chocolate shake. I've wanted a meal like this for years.

A handful even suggests eliminating routine screening and treatment for many people told to go on low-fat diets and take cholesterol-lowering drugs.

Right on, Doc. I hear you.

Dinnertime is going to be something to look forward to again.

A juicy steak would be nice . . . not too well done . . . let's see some red when the knife slices through. And a baked potato. Butter or sour cream? You read the report; let's have both. And put bleu cheese on that salad. A chilled glass of red wine will help burn up some of that choleste . . . But, hey, we don't have to worry about that anymore, do we?

In a pig's eye we don't!

161

No matter how tasty that eggs and bacon—gosh, I forgot to ask for gravy!—sounds, we better pass on it. A bowl of Wheaties will be fine, thank you, with low-fat milk. Skim milk is fine or nothing more than 2 percent.

I really, really was looking forward to that cheeseburger. But I can mentally picture those clogged arteries—plugged solid with what looks an awful lot like melted cheese. I'll settle for tuna salad. And maybe some cottage cheese and fruit.

Well, the surgeon DID say to forget the diet every once in a while and live it up with a real meal. But chicken or turkey will be fine again, or perhaps some fish. As long as it's not out of the Ohio River.

I just got carried away for a few minutes, all because of another study.

You know how those studies go. A few weeks ago, the value of milk was questioned. White bread has been challenged. Decaf coffee or regular?

If enough doctors study enough things long enough, someone is bound to come up with the results someone wants to hear. The study will be published in some medical journal, the researchers' egos will grow and in a few months the study will be forgotten.

Never mind how much damage the findings may cause some people. They shouldn't have abandoned their cholesterol-reducing diet in the first place, they will be scolded.

Why do we even read such reports? Because we devour every word that is written on the subject of cholesterol, blockages and heart attacks in hopes of finding some clue to help us live longer.

Forget cholesterol counts? No thanks.

And just for your information, Mr. Medical Researcher, on the very day the results of your study were published in nearly every newspaper in the country, I got a report from my doctor on my cholesterol.

After 29 days on a new (for me) cholesterol-reducing drug, my numbers dropped 43 points to the lowest level it has been in years.

That may not mean anything to you and it may not mean that I'll live any longer or won't have a heart attack tomorrow.

But it thrilled me almost to death, (which would defeat the purpose, wouldn't it?). It made me happy and my doctors happy and if those arteries could talk, they would probably thank me for reducing the cholesterol they have to carry every day.

October, 1992

Take two and call me in the morning

The friendly people at my phavorite pharmacy gave me a nice little gift not too long ago.

162

It's a pill carrier. The pharmacy pholks know I take a lot of pills because they sell them to me. Lots of them.

The pill carrier is a fraction over six inches long, an inch and a quarter wide and three-quarters of an inch deep. It's divided into seven compartments clearly marked S, M, T, W, T, F, S and that is fine as long as you don't get the two S's and two T's mixed up.

There also are little tiny markings in the lower right corner of each compartment which I strongly suspect are the first letters of each day of the week in Braille. I don't know for sure and most certainly hope I never have to find out. If that is, indeed, what those markings are, then I have an additional new measure of respect for those who have to use them to make sure they're taking their pills on the proper day.

There are many, many of these pill carriers on the shelves at your drugstore, all designed with the pill-swallowing public's convenience in mind. Mine is first class, for sure, especially since it was a gift. Absolutely phree. A little token of appreciation for giving this particular drugstore my business.

But I have never used it. Not once. It's just not big enough.

What I need is a pill carrier that is large enough to hold 20 pills a day but has each daily compartment divided into three sections marked M, N and N for morning, noon and night. That still would leave the potential problem of getting the two N's confused, but some things you just have put up with.

The best solution, perhaps, would be to get the pharmacist to combine all these medicines into three big pills that could be taken M, N and N. But they undoubtedly would be too big to swallow.

My pills are a colorful bunch, something you would expect from an interior decorator instead of a drugstore.

The newest—and most expensive! one—is a cholesterol phighter that's sort of a robin's egg blue with just a hint of tiny white specks all over it. It's a once-a-day pill that replaced pretty green and white transparent capsules with a red stripe around the midsection. Inside were hundreds, maybe thousands, of multicolored little time-release things. These were taken twice a day.

I don't know what the others are for, except that all are for heart-related problems. They include:

* A peach-colored round pill that I take three times a day, unless I happen to drop it on the bed spread which is the same color and makes the dropped pill nearly impossible to find.

* Two a day that are the same color as Cleveland Browns helmets. These may be some kind of coated aspirins, but I'm not sure. It's really not important that I know as long as the doctor and pharmacist do.

* A little white football-shaped pill that is broken in half

163

and taken twice a day.

* A big white, or sometimes yellow, thing that would almost choke a horse. Once a day. I think it may have something to do with potassium, whatever that is. It either puts in potassium or takes it out, whichever the doctor wants.

* Two little oblong mint green things that make me trot to the bathroom every 10 minutes or so and are real trouble if we're going to be in the car very long.

* Something that looks like a partly deflated chocolate football, three times a day.

* A nondescript little white thing that says 313 on one side, which might be a good number to play in the daily lottery; I've never tried it. Three a day.

* Three round Boston cream (the same color as our walls) pills with more lottery numbers on them but I don't remember what they are.

There also are two vitamin pills a day, but they don't count because you don't have to have a prescription to get them.

Naturally, you can't take this many pills a day without having a drug problem. I have one. My drug problem is that I forget to take my pills. Twelve years of popping them three times a day and I still forget.

Wonder if I can get some kind of memory pill?

February, 1994

Mr. Coffee loses his Mrs. Olson

Coffee always has been one of the most important parts of life at our house. It's the same way in many of your homes as well, isn't it? Cut your finger and what comes out is as likely to be black—or maybe with cream—as it is red, right?

For many, many years coffee was a three-pots-a-day habit. There was the mandatory morning eye opener, about three cups. Then another pot at suppertime (that was before we started calling the evening meal dinner) and finally a smaller one, perhaps two cups apiece before bedtime.

That was in the days when late-night TV meant the likes of Jerry Lester and Dagmar, Steve Allen's zanies and Jack Paar. Johnny Carson was still a game-show host and David Letterman was a kid in school in Indiana.

Of course, during the day there were countless cups of that vending machine stuff that masquerades as coffee.

Keep us awake? Gosh, no. And it still doesn't. The woman I drink coffee with can set her cup down and be dozing before it reaches the saucer.

Like many of you, my coffee usually was accompanied by a cigarette. Also preceded and followed by one, too.

164

Then, a few days after Christmas—the worst possible time to be in a hospital—in 1967, a doctor took a pack of L&M's out of my robe pocket, pried away another hidden in my hand and in his sternest doctor voice said, "You can't have that! You can't have another one as long as you live."

Pretty heavy stuff to lay on someone who usually was working on his fourth pack at the end of every day.

But there was always coffee, good old hot, black coffee to keep us going. Walk into any truck stop, restaurant or coffee shop and there we sit, millions of us, sipping cup after cup after cup.

We could give up cigarettes—and there was only one after that winter day in 1967—and live happily ever after.

Wrong! No way.

You see, your friendly family doctor, cardiologist, surgeon and all the others they work with have this diabolical plan to take away, one by one, all of the good things in life.

You have to cut down on this, they say, and that isn't good for you. No red meat, no bacon and eggs, no hamburgers, no fried food, no cheese. Hey, what is there left to eat?

The new word in our vocabulary was cholesterol. Our 1951-model dictionary offers only a three-line definition. Our 1976 edition gave it seven lines. But neither indicated anything harmful about this newest dirty word. The newest 1988 dictionary at the library has only five lines devoted to cholesterol, but one of them warns that "if present in the blood in excessive amounts, a factor in atherosclerosis."

And we all know what that means, don't we? Clogged arteries. Bypass surgery. Heart attacks. Don't buy anything at the grocery store without reading the labels. No meat unless it swims or flies. Oh, for the good old days when we were ignorant of all the health risks. Ignorant but happy.

But we still have our coffee. No one has said we can't have a cup of coffee or two or three. Often more. One of the men in white coats did recommend about 10 years ago that we switch to unleaded, better known as decaffeinated. No problem.

But, if you'll pardon the cliche, all good things must come to an end.

A few weeks ago, the woman I drink coffee with was advised to give it up. No more coffee, regular or decaf. Not even just one cup in the morning. No tea. No colas. Quit right now, he ordered, not Monday, not next week or next month.

I don't have to quit. I go to a different man in a white coat. I still can drink my mountain grown, good to the last drop. And when the last drop is gone, pour another cup.

But it isn't easy. It's really tough to enjoy a cup of coffee when someone is sitting across the table with eyes as sad as a Saint Bernard or a basset hound.

It's a tough job, but somebody's got to do it. And I volunteer.

October, 1989

Looking for the Smith Brothers

You'll probably think I'm crazy for saying (actually, writing) this, but I'm looking forward to the cold and flu season.

For one thing, I've already had my flu shot. For another, I feel pretty certain I already have reached my quota of coughing for the year. Perhaps next year, too.

And if that is the case, the next few months should be comparatively quiet and peaceful around our house.

Is there anything more aggravating and uncomfortable than a coughing siege? I'm sure there is, but for my sake please answer "No" so I can continue without interruption.

Coughing also is embarrassing. A cough will start tickling in your throat and working its way slowly up your neck. You can purse your lips tightly together in hopes of suppressing it, but it never works. All at once your mouth flies open and out comes a sound something like "Uh huh, uh huh, uh huh" or even "Arf, arf, arf," much like a young beagle on the trail of a rabbit.

That's usually followed by a long wheezing sound in a futile attempt to clear your throat and eject whatever caused the tickling in the first place.

It's embarrassing. And it never works.

I've always coughed a lot. I can remember as a kid being told, "All you have to do is look out the window and you catch pneumonia."

That probably is just a bit of exaggeration, but I did have a lot of bad colds that my parents and grandparents diagnosed as pneumonia. The worst was when I was about 4 years old (Wow! That sure was a long time ago.) and the family doctor supposedly said she had done all she could do and it was now out of her hands.

Then I remember waking up to the overwhelming smell of fried onions that were being placed on my chest in almost blistering poultices. They did the trick, but ever since when I order a hamburger I ask them to "Hold the onions."

I've had pneumonia countless times since. The last was in 1980 and a doctor in Kentucky gave me a pneumonia shot. Every year that passes makes that one bout with a needle the best medical bargain I have ever found.

But I didn't have pneumonia or even a cold this summer when the Great Coughing Spell of 1993 began. It was on April 30 and we were on a camping trip. First came the irritating throat tickle. Then a slight cough. The next day was worse. So was the next and the next and the next ad nauseam.

I took shots. I took antibiotics. I took a lot of naps. Long naps. But they always were interrupted by frequent and violent bed-shaking coughing.

"There's a lot of it going around," I was told. "It's some kind of virus."

Misery loves company and I found plenty. One friend couldn't speak above a whisper for much of the summer and although her husband wouldn't say so publicly, he loved every minute of it.

Cough drops didn't help. That was something I always looked forward to as a kid, because in reality cough drops became the candy you weren't allowed to have when you were sick. Usually, they were those black licorice Smith Brothers brand with the pictures of Trade and Mark on the box.

My coughing and that of several acquaintances went on for most of the summer. I still do occasionally, but now it usually is dismissed with "Are you still doing that?" as if it is a cheap bid for attention.

All of us coughers and hackers finally gained a little credibility in late summer from an unexpected source. Neon Deion Sanders of the Atlanta Braves and the Atlanta Falcons, depending on the season, was placed on his team's disabled list because of a chronic cough.

How a germ or a virus ever got through all his gold chains is beyond me, but it happened. Deion was diagnosed as having an upper respiratory infection. That sounds much more impressive than coughing spells, doesn't it?

October, 1993

The A, B, C's of health care

"I don't believe this!" wailed the woman who pays the bills and balances the check book—not to mention doing the cooking, cleaning, laundry, gardening and similar chores—at our house.

"These bills are so screwed up that I don't know whether to laugh or cry."

Her desk, which even on good days looks much like a small landfill minus the flies, had spread to the nearby bed. The bed now was covered by a spread of papers. All had to do with requests for money.

The money was requested by: A. An insurance company. B. A doctor's office. C. A hospital. The money they requested was: A. $270.19. B. $25. C. $478.10.

Believe me, the woman who pays the bills and does all that other stuff pays our bills on time. B may disagree, but we'll get to that later.

167

Why, many of you are asking by now, is he telling us all about his overdue bills?

Because, as most of you know, anyone who has ever done business with A. An insurance company. B. A doctor's office. C. A hospital most likely have had a similar experience. Or, probably, experiences.

A, B and C will not be identified. No way. They have ways of getting even. A can cut off my insurance. B can cut off anything he darn well pleases. C can refuse to give me a bed where I can recover from what B did because it knows A won't pay the bills.

The only thing we can do is pay their bills, whether we agree with them or not.

Here's our case:

A was submitted a claim for $1,126.46 for prescription drugs in 1989. A disallowed $61.33, leaving us entitled to 80 percent reimbursement of the remainder, or $852.10.

Many of you have traveled this same route, haven't you? OK, so far, so good.

But then, for some unexplained reason, A decided to break up the claim into two or three. The first part was paid. Fine. The second part was paid, too. That's also fine. The next envelope should bring the third part, right?

Wrong!

The third part brought a testy request for the return of $270.19, which A claimed it had overpaid us. It seems that someone working for A had noted two payments were close to the same amount and concluded we had been paid twice. If A had paid the claim in one amount as submitted in the first place, this mess would never have happened.

This all started in June. Since then we have spent a tidy amount for postage, phone calls and copies of all of our drug bills. And we're no closer to a resolution than in the beginning. The year is almost over. It soon will be time to seek reimbursement for 1990's prescriptions. Do we dare?

B surprised us about three months ago with a request for $25 it said was owed since April, 1989. Lack of payment had been discovered in an annual audit completed in June, 1990, we were told. Why, we wondered, hadn't it been discovered in the audit a year before?

We don't make it a practice to pay requests for money that appear out of the blue, 14 or 15 months after the fact and without documentation that we hadn't indeed paid it. Besides, the bill-payer, checkbook-balancer etc. also is a pretty good record-keeper. Her records show we made the required office call payment back in April, 1989, and the remainder should have been filed by B with A. Our bulging file of records from A show B apparently never did.

168

But C did. We found that out only a couple of weeks ago when A informed us it couldn't pay C $478.10 for surgery performed in November, 1989, "until we receive a reply to our request for information from the provider." C already had been paid $2,046.19 by A.

It was at this point that the bill-payer etc. couldn't decide whether to laugh or cry. The choice was easy. Pass that box of tissues this way when you're finished.

November, 1990

One of God's special children

This is a thanksgiving story, even though the big bird checked out a few days ago.

Few of you know any of the people involved, except The Great Healer who wrote the happy ending. But you don't have to know them; after all, it could have been one of your children or grandchildren.

The cast of characters includes a young couple from Alabama and their 13-month-old son, Nathan. There are two older children, Joshua, 5, and Lacey, going on 3, but this story is about Nathan.

Their Mamma was a journalism student of mine in the early '80s. She was majoring in broadcast journalism and had the kind of face that was meant to be on a TV screen.

Unfortunately, she didn't have the voice to go with the face. She is from Georgia. Stir that kind of accent with four years of Alabama and . . . well, you know. It's pretty to listen to in conversation, but stretches the words out 'way too long for delivering news briefs.

Mamma was a character, using the word in a complimentary sort of way. In Alabama, we used to say "She's a mess," an often-used expression which was interpreted to mean she was a very nice girl who was fun to have around. In the school of journalism, we called her Spacy Lacey. That was her maiden name.

She eventually changed her major to something else— education, I think—graduated and married an accountant.

Along came Joshua, one of the handsomest kids you ever laid eyes on, then Lacey, who'll surely be a replica of her mother. Nathan was a good-looking baby, too. Except when he turned blue.

And that was frequently during the first year of his life.

The couple took their baby to Children's Hospital in Birmingham when he was two weeks old. Doctors checked out his heart to make sure he had adequate circulation and pronounced him OK.

169

But interns who looked in on him wondered aloud why his breathing was so loud. Doctors said he would outgrow it.

Nathan was back in Birmingham two weeks later for treatment of another illness and again his loud breathing was questioned. And again it was decided that condition was only temporary.

When Nathan was six weeks old, he was taken to the University of South Alabama Hospital in Mobile. Doctors there discovered that his epiglottis—a cartilage at the root of the tongue that keeps food from entering the windpipe—was occasionally inhaled into his windpipe, causing Nathan to turn blue.

Nathan was put on a monitor that would warn his parents if he stopped breathing. But after eight months, Nathan became so active he could get the monitor cords wrapped around his neck, posing another threat to his young life.

A couple of weeks ago, Nathan went into the hospital again to have a double hernia repaired. The surgeon decided to check his breathing problem more closely. A pediatric ear, nose and throat specialist used an instrument that probed inside his throat and revealed that Nathan's vocal cords were fused together. That left only a tiny opening for breathing.

The parents were told few babies survive such a condition and that it is one of the causes attributed to sudden infant death syndrome.

Plans were made immediately to bring Nathan to Cincinnati Children's Hospital (in Cincinnati, Ohio) for a rare surgery to separate his vocal cords. Even if he survived, his parents were told, there was the risk of severing the cords, leaving him unable to speak.

Mamma and Daddy left their other two children in Alabama and flew to Cincinnati with Nathan. They were told he could be in the hospital as long as three weeks—into December.

Surgeons again explained the risks involved and inserted a small lens into Nathan's throat, the same procedure that discovered the fused vocal cords in Birmingham.

What they saw this time was different, however. Nathan's vocal cords had separated themselves.

"The doctor said he couldn't explain it," his Mamma told me on the phone. "He said it was just a miracle. Nathan is one of God's special children."

Amen.

December, 1991

13-Happy Holidaze

My favorite holiday is

Christ . . ., no, it's the Fourth

of Jul . . ., but Thanksgiving

is filling as well as fulfilling.

I guess I just love them all.

Even Arbor Day.

Two Christmas gifts we are happy without

Thank you, Santa.

And Mom and Dad, our children, brothers and sisters, friends . . . whoever was responsible for the many gifts that were placed under, around or anywhere in the vicinity of our Christmas tree.

We thank you not only for the many beautiful, useful and practical things you saw fit to bestow upon us, but also for a couple of things that you wisely chose to forget. There were several things that the Head of the House and I wanted very badly. And we even received one or two of them.

There also were a few that we fervently hoped not to see when we came downstairs on the morning of Dec. 25. We were reminded of them constantly. They were on our TV screens daily. They took up space in our newspapers and appeared prominently in gift catalogs. They were in all the stores. They haunted us day and night.

"They," in ladies-before-gentlemen order, were:

1. A breadmaker.
2. Silk boxer shorts.

"I don't want a breadmaker," declared the woman who toasts my bread. "If I get a breadmaker for Christmas, I'm telling you right now I'm going to take it back."

She was reacting to diversionary hints that a breadmaker might indeed find its way down our chimney or whatever route such gifts take into the house. The hints were just that, diversionary. I didn't want to give her a breadmaker any more than she wanted to receive one.

I knew what would happen if she did get the dreaded appliance. We would be sitting around in the evening, watching TV commercials or reading newspaper ads about breadmakers, and I would say, "I'm a little hungry. I think I'll go make a sandwich."

She would reply: "Why don't you just eat a cookie or a handful of pretzels. If you want a sandwich, I'll have to bake some bread."

Hey, when I want a sandwich, I want it now. I don't want to have to wait for the yeast to rise, the flour to settle and whatever you have to do to bake bread. That's why we have bakeries and grocery stores. But I will have a cookie. And maybe just a couple of pretzels.

The ads and commercials are so tempting. "Enjoy the unbeatable taste of homemade breads!" they say, ending every sentence with an exclamation point.

"The breadmaker is easy to use! Makes a 1 1/2 pound loaf in a non-stick pan! Five bread settings, crust color selector, four dough settings!"

All those bread and dough settings sound a bit confusing. But the crust color selector came within a crumb of hooking us. We wondered if every other slice could be a different shade of golden brown. Or maybe something that would match the kitchen curtains.

But the promise—or perhaps it was more of a threat—was no joking matter to the woman who really was beginning to fear that she would become the owner of one.

"I swear," she vowed, "if I get a breadmaker, I'll take it back. I just want to eat bread, I don't want to make it."

I felt the same way about the 100 percent silk boxer shorts that seemed to be at the corner of the aisle in nearly every store I entered this season. They didn't turn me on for two reasons: Most of the ones I saw were outrageously expensive and I always felt that silk undies should be in my wife's dresser drawers, not mine.

"Twenty dollars for a pair of underwear?" I bellowed loudly enough to be heard in the sporting goods and automotive department at the far end of the department store. "If I pay 20 bucks for a pair of shorts, I blankety-blank sure am not going to wear anything over them. I'll want the whole world to know what I have on."

And the patterns and names they put on underwear nowadays. It's not like the long johns some of us had to wear years ago, causing permanent embarrassment when we had to go to gym class and the teams were divided into shirts and skins.

One manufacturer put out a line picturing bottles of hot sauce, onions, jalapeno peppers and carrying a recipe for Bayou Baked Beans on the tag. How could a guy keep his cool wearing such a pair of hot pants?

There was underwear called "Bottoms Out" and "Reckless," prompting the woman I was shopping with to lay down the law: "I wouldn't allow my husband or son to leave the house wearing shorts with those labels on them."

Thanks, Santa, for not bringing us exactly what we didn't want.

January, 1995

I can change my mind . . . and my shorts, too

I have changed my mind. More often than not, we think of that as a woman's prerogative—whether it's changing her mind or yours—but this time, I'm going to do it.

What I am changing my mind about is rather personal. But inasmuch as I mentioned it in this same space a couple of weeks or so ago, I feel somewhat obligated to mention it here again.

I'm changing my mind bout silk underwear.

If you don't recall, I'll refresh your memory. I told you that for a few weeks before Christmas, my wife and I had made no secret of the fact there were two things we hoped we wouldn't receive as gifts. She didn't want a breadmaker and I didn't want silk underwear.

Her main reason for not wanting a breadmaker was that she would much rather simply eat bread, not make it. I had several reasons for not wanting silk underwear.

The most important, I suppose, was that it was pretty expensive. Buy me a three-pack or a six-pack of cotton briefs and I'll get along fine, thank you. I also felt that silk underwear was kind of—forgive me for saying this, all of you big husky guys who wear it—effeminate.

There's a third reason, too. I just knew that the first time they were laundered, my silk drawers would wind up in the drawer where she keeps her silk drawers. I just didn't want all that confusion when I stepped out of the shower and was looking for some clean underwear.

But, as I said in the first line, I changed my mind.

The reason I did was a little catalog that came in the mail the other day. It was from Winter Silks, which offers "Quality silk clothing at factory direct prices." Winter Silks even has an 800 number so you can order 24 hours a day, which would be especially nice when I step out of the shower and all my silk drawers are in someone else's drawer.

Actually, the catalog wasn't from Winter Silks. It was from someone else who had received the catalog. They had cut their own address off the catalog and mailed it to me with this stick-on note attached:

"Jim—See pg 26, 34, 40, 51. Very you."

"Very you" was double underlined. Now wouldn't you think that someone who knows me that well would have signed the note? But he or she didn't.

I liked what I found in the catalog. On 26 were Palace Paisley silk boxers with a matching robe in unisex sizes. We could get matching robes, which would be nice if my wife didn't get flour all over hers while making bread.

On 34 were seven pairs of silk briefs, including one G-string model. Every pair of those would wind up in the wrong drawer. On 40 were his and her Adventurous Silk Aviator Scarfs. I'll pass on those. But I was turned on by the Stylish 100% Silk Khaki Pants For Men on 51. Very me. With my own double underline.

There were several other things in the catalog that I liked. The Pure Silk V-Neck Long Johns (for men and women) in Navy or Cream were very attractive, for instance.

Same goes for the sporty silk jackets, cardigans, slip-overs and even a blazer on 54 and 55. There were a few nice silk ties, too. But I rarely wear a tie anymore since I've retired. I nearly choke myself getting one tied now and almost do it again when I'm taking it off.

This is a really nice catalog. And I haven't even looked at the women's pages yet.

But my wife remains adamant, which is a polite way of saying stubborn. She still doesn't want a breadmaker.

January, 1995

For whom the Christmases toll

Excuse me.

If you could spare a moment at this most-hectic time of year, I'd like to ask what you may think is a wee-bit-too personal question:

Does it seem as if it takes longer to get ready for Christmas than it used to? Are you so stressed out you don't give a wassail bowl if you get the last few cards addressed and it doesn't bother you a bit that the string of lights at the very top of the tree quit burning last night?

OK, so that is two questions. That just helps sharpen the point I'm trying to make.

At our house, the woman I deck the halls with and I exchange weary glances over rolls of wrapping paper and ask each other:

How did we ever get ready for the holidays when we were both working, had children at home and felt that it bordered on blasphemy not to bake cookies in preparation for the BIG DAY.

That was 'way back when we frequently would spend the better part of a day looking for a live tree that was as close to perfect as could be. Now we simply reach into a box and pull out a fake one made of metal and some kind of synthetics.

There was more too: Far more (and rowdier) Christmas parties, 250-mile round trips for visits and passing parties with parents, brothers and sisters, nieces and nephews and anyone else who chanced to wander in.

After the kids got a little older, it became necessary to hurry to Lexington about this time—and even later—to bring them and all their worldly possessions home from the University of Kentucky. The return trip, providing no one flunked out, was only about two weeks later.

We did all that and perhaps more in the true spirit of the season . . . Ho, ho, ho! and all that goes with it.

Could we do that now? Of course not. You've been sniffing too many poinsettias or something. Get real.

So what's the problem? Could it be age? No, of course not. You're just as old as you feel.

Well, maybe that has a little to do with it.

Perhaps.

Of course! That has to be it.

Why else would it take nearly three days to get all the outside lights in place? Could be those strings of lights that have teeny, tiny fuses so small you almost need tweezers to pick them up with and a magnifying glass to replace it. Three hands would help.

And still addressing cards and writing notes on the 20th of December? That's the price you pay for moving every five or 10 years and having dear friends in several states. It's an occupational hazard. We've got to tackle that chore next year as soon as Halloween is over.

Shopping takes longer, too. Once upon a time we could wait until mid-month, then take one day and do it all. But weary, old legs can't carry those extra pounds. They once were much younger and the bodies they hauled were trimmer and oh, so much slimmer.

There were no grandchildren to shop for, either. We're now looking for things that didn't even exist when their parents were their age.

Candy? Cookies? Not from Mother Joseph's kitchen. If it's cookies you want, go to the bakery or the grocery store.

But I do miss those homemade bourbon balls. Take the lid off a well-filled container and the aroma was . . . well, almost intoxicating.

There was a standing rule at our house: Nobody eats any of Mom's bourbon balls if they were going to be driving soon. They'd flunk the Breathalyzer test for certain.

December, 1992

'Dear Santa: About that train . . .'

DEAR SANTA:

Surprise! I bet you didn't expect to hear from me, did you? It's been quite a while since I last wrote to you. But I had a little time to kill, and who better to kill it with than you?

Now I've done it, haven't I? By starting my letter as I did, you probably think I'm just attempting to butter you up and score a few points. Well, you're absolutely right; I am. You might not really understand what I mean when I say butter you up. Modern-day folks use a different verb in that infinitive, but I don't think it's one you would approve. I sure don't want to get in trouble with you at this time of year.

As I said earlier, it's been some time since I last wrote to you. I suspect I was about 8 years old—I was a slow learner—at

176

the time, and as I recall, you didn't exactly come through the way I had hoped you would. But that was back in 1938, so I doubt if very many kids got what they wanted that year. Looking back, I realize we were lucky you stopped at our house at all.

But you always did, and for that I will always be grateful.

I kind of lost touch with you for the next 15 years until you started making toy drops at hour house again. By the way, you really goofed that year; 1953, I think it was. You delivered a couple of battery-operated toys to my namesake and forgot to bring any batteries! Do you know how difficult it is to find batteries at 3 o'clock in the morning? Stores and service stations didn't stay open 24 hours then.

Still, you and I got along pretty well over the years. My three kids were slow learners, too. Or pretty good actors. Probably the reason things went so smoothly is that when one of my runny-nosed youngsters asked for something that was too sophisticated, too dangerous or too expensive, you saw me in the background, shaking my head in the negative. I still owe you for that. All the cookies and milk left under the tree couldn't begin to settle that old debt. You should have eaten them; they were good.

But, hey, I know you're busy. You have miles to travel, so I'll get to the point:

Do you think you could bring me an electric train for Christmas?

You brought me one in 1935, but I really wasn't old enough to play with it. I think Dad did, though. He's probably the one that wanted it in the first place. Mom died before next Christmas and I went to live with my grandparents. I don't know what happened to my (and Dad's) electric train.

In 1938, Dad married a new Mom and we were all back together at Christmastime. I asked for an electric train that year, but there was one hang-up: We didn't have electricity. So you brought me a windup. Dad played with it before I even knew you had been to our house. It woke me up, but I still acted surprised the next morning. I just didn't write you any more letters.

Whoa! Hold it, Santa, I can't believe I'm doing this. As good as you have been to me, my children and my grandchildren, here I am trying to prey on your sympathy for an electric engine, three or four cars, a transformer and a few pieces of track. Shame on me!

If you know when I am sleeping and you know when I'm awake, and if you know if I've been bad or good, you also know I'm too old to be crawling around on the floor trying to get derailed cars back on the track. Forget my train. Give it to some kid with a Dad young enough to play with it.

As usual, there will be cookies and milk under the tree. Or

at least a few crumbs.

—JIM(MY) JOSEPH
December, 1995

You have to do it by the book

"Where are you going with those Christmas cards? You can't mail them like that," scolded the woman I lick envelopes and postage stamps with. Her tone of voice was that which the Creator reserved for wives, grade school teachers, drill sergeants and an editor or two I have worked for.

Why not? They've all got stamps on them. Ernie (our friendly local mail carrier) won't bring it back with a postage-due label on it like that big fat envelope I tried to sneak through for a quarter last week. Besides, I thought the post office would make them pay at the other end.

"I know they all have stamps on them," replied the woman who checks and sometimes double-checks such things. "I checked. But look what you did. We can't mail Christmas cards addressed like this."

Why not (pardon the redundancy; it's all I could think of at the moment)? They have stamps on them, they have return address labels and I checked the ZIP Codes.

"That's not what I'm talking about," she continued, which she is very good at it when she's talking; it runs in her family. "Look what you have done! You've addressed them all in red or green ink."

Sure did. Neat, huh. Real Christmasy. I goofed on a couple, though. That red writing is a little tough to read on a red envelope. And I may have used the green pen on a green envelope or two, but I think I got most of them red on green or green on red like I should have.

"Dummy, you're supposed to use black ink," she said in her best wife-teacher-drill-sergeant tone. It didn't sound editorish because there was no profanity. "And you're supposed to type or print the addresses."

That came as a shock. Miss Manners frowns on typing addresses on cards and personal notes. Miss Manners frowns on a lot of things I do all the time. So does my wife. But this is the first time I ever got a dressing-down over how I addressed mail.

Since when?

"Since we got that thing from the U.S. Postal Service, that's when. Didn't you read it? That's all you do anyhow is read. Why don't you read something that's important sometime?"

Is that all there was to it? Just print addresses in black ink?

"No," she answered, "there was a lot more. It told us how to address our mail for the best mail service. It said the post office has installed new facilities and high-speed electronic scanning

178

equipment to give us faster delivery."

Funny, you live with someone for nearly 40 years and it's the first time I ever knew she had even a clue how the post office works.

"Look at these!" she ordered, fanning through the green and red envelopes I had carelessly failed to address with the preferred basic black. "You didn't even use the right state abbreviations. You spelled out Ohio. You abbreviated Alabama as Ala.!"

The next time she opens her mouth, there may be a little editor mixed in with wife, teacher, drill sergeant. I better be careful. But I've always spelled out Ohio. I learned that from The Associated Press Stylebook more than 40 years ago. I've always spelled out Texas, Utah, Iowa and Idaho, too. I'd spell out Alaska, Hawaii and Maine as well, but I never write anyone who lives in those states.

And Ala. is the correct abbreviation for Alabama. It could be the abbreviation for Alaska, too, but Alabama has been a state longer so Alaska got frozen out. Ha, Ha. That's a joke, get it?

Only an icy glare. Then she showed me the thing the post office sent. It has its own abbreviations for all 50 states. Can you imagine someone being in such a hurry that he can't take time to spell out Ohio?

And why does CO. stand for Colorado instead of Connecticut? Why isn't Maine MA. instead of ME.? Because MA. is Massachusetts, that's why, although it could just as easily be Maryland. MS. could be Mississippi, Missouri or a woman who doesn't want you to know if she's a Miss or a Mrs. And it goes on and on.

Next year, I'm not sending any Christmas cards.

December, 1989

Go soak a noodle, Ann

Dear Ann Landers:

How is it you punish yourself when you give someone a rare bum answer? Twenty lashes with a wet noodle? Yeah, that's it. Well go soak a couple, because you blew one the other day.

Actually, you've blown it more than once because the column I'm referring to has been repeated several times, I'm certain.

It's the one in which a letter writer takes to task the people who compose and then have the nerve to mail Christmas newsletters.

"I am galled," your reader wrote (and no doubt she is and it probably has nothing at all to do with newsletters; more than likely her underwear is too tight), "by those who portray glowing

179

pictures of affluence and success."

She gripes that they mail "those interminable newsletters to everyone who has sent them so much as a rummage sale announcement during the past year." Then she gave a most exaggerated example of a Christmas newsletter and followed it with the kind of letter of failure and poverty she would like to send "to all the bores who have been sending us theirs."

It was all so cutesy wootsie.

You made it worse by answering a letter from Your Fan in Tokyo who asked that it be repeated by saying that every November you get "hundreds of requests for that column."

Hey, Ann, baby, how about the thousands, even millions of us who don't request it.

I have no idea who wrote the original letter or where that person lives, but there's a better than even chance it was from a "Very Sad and Unfulfilled Person in Dullsville."

Surely she and "Your Fan in Tokyo" have had something good happen to them at least once in their lives that made them want to tell the whole world about it. And if they couldn't do that, they'd at least like to spread the word among a few friends and acquaintances.

Apparently they haven't.

They sound like the kind of people who are so boring and lead such blah lives they hate to see the dawn of a new day. They're miserable people who can't stand to see others be happy and achieve even the slightest bit of success. There's a name for such people, but Charles Dickens has already given it to Ebeneezer Scrooge.

We get several Christmas newsletters each year. But they're nothing like the kind your reader sent to you, Ann.

They usually tell us of new arrivals, mostly grandchildren but we do have a few friends young enough to send pictures of their children. Every once in a while we hear of a job promotion or something like that. But in the last few years, most have been quite happy to be able to tell us they still have a job.

There's always one newsletter that is downright hilarious from a guy who puts a great deal of time, effort and affection (what the heck, call it love) into his annual effort.

As for any from people whom your first writer would call bores, Ann, there is no one holding a gun on us to force us to read them. If we ever get any, and we haven't yet, we will boldly and courageously crumple them into a tiny ball and hurl them toward the nearest waste basket.

Gosh, Ann, I really feel sorry for people such as the one who wrote the original letter and "Your Fan in Tokyo."

'Tis the season to be jolly, and all they can find to do is gripe about someone's newsletter. They're pathetic.

'Fess up, Ann. Was that first letter for real? Or did you fake it to help fill a page?

—Phil Spayse, Ohio
December, 1992

What goes up must come down

The tree still looks pretty good.

Unusually good, considering it's the day after Christmas and it's been up since Nov. 26. Of course, the grandchildren won't arrive until today. The tree probably won't look very good by tomorrow.

Getting the tree up early was a trick we picked up back in the mid-'70s when our two daughters were attending the University of Kentucky. When they came home for Thanksgiving, we took advantage of their brief presence to get the decorating done.

We had to. We were both working then and there were three trees to be trimmed. There was a big live one in the family room in the basement, a smaller artificial one in the living room and an aluminum one in the upstairs hall.

It probably wasn't really aluminum. But it looked like aluminum. Do people still use trees like that? Why did they ever use them in the first place? They don't even look like Christmas trees. They're shaped like a Christmas tree and decorated like a Christmas tree and if you've been good all year, there may be presents under it like a Christmas tree. But a Christmas tree that looks like aluminum is just a fraud perpetrated by scheming marketers who know we'll buy just about anything.

Gosh, that was nearly 20 years ago. Neither of us is working anymore. But we still take advantage of one daughter's presence on Thanksgiving weekend to get some decorating done. She'll wise up someday, but until she does, we've got a pretty good thing going.

There's only one tree now. It's artificial. The small artificial one is now in a box in the basement. The aluminum-looking one is gone to wherever castoff trees go, perhaps to hell where their scheming marketers will join them someday.

We chose a 7-foot artificial tree more for safety's sake than any other reason. Have you ever seen how quickly a live tree can flare up if ignited? It's scary.

The artificial tree is the target of scorn from an 8-year-old grandson whose father is a tree farmer. To him, it's a fake.

Our tree should look pretty good. Heaven knows, we've had plenty of practice decorating it . . . four times this year alone!

We were making pretty good progress the first time. The last string of lights was being placed on the lowest fake branches when the woman in charge took a third step on a two-step stool and went head first into the tree.

181

The tree remained standing as she was helped to her feet and checked for scratches and bruises.

Then, without so much as a warning cry of "Timberrrrrr!", the tree did a slow-motion fall to the floor.

We regrouped. Several hours later, the job was competed a second time. Well done.

But it needed moved back closer to the wall. I stretched out on my back on the floor where I could reach the holder and move it. As I looked up through lights, countless ornaments and fake pine, a hand reached through and pulled on the metal trunk. Down it went a second time.

"It's the @&#$*&%! holder!" I complained. "I told you last year we needed a new one. I'm going after one."

But the woman in charge had a better idea. "Let's use the holder for the patio umbrella," she suggested. "It has a bigger base and won't fall over as easily."

"It won't work," I protested. "The table helps hold up the umbrella. The tree doesn't have a table. There are only two bolts and that isn't enough."

We tried the umbrella holder anyway. As predicted, the tree went over again. That's three times, and Christmas was nearly a month away.

The tree spent the night leaning against the couch, surrounded by fallen pretty things.

I was in a nearby store minutes after it opened the next morning. The first new holder, exactly like the old one, was no better; the four gripping bolts didn't line up properly. The second new holder did the job. It has eight gripping bolts to hold the tree in place.

But have you ever lifted a fully decorated (almost) tree straight up out of one holder and sat it down into another? Take my word: Don't try it.

After all it's been through, the tree looks pretty good. Not one ornament was broken.

December, 1993

Let there be lights until spring

"Hey," said the voice at the other end of the phone, "don't you think it's about time to take down those Christmas lights?"

No introduction, no hello, no how are you? or any other foreplay. Just right into criticism of the timing of the holiday decorations at our house.

Well, I replied, I expect we'll get around to it in a few days. Or maybe next week or the week after, providing the weather warms up a little. What's the problem?

"No problem," my caller continued. "You're the one who's

paying the electric bills. And they are pretty, even if you do the same thing every year. But I seem to recall you writing something back around Thanksgiving about people putting lights up so early. What's the difference between someone having their lights burning so early and you having yours on so late?"

Gee, thanks, I told him, I really appreciate your reading and remembering something I wrote nearly two months ago. But I think you may have missed my point.

What I was trying to get across is that it seems as if Thanksgiving is becoming our forgotten holiday. We put up Halloween decorations at the end of September, take them down during the first week of November and replace them with Christmas lights.

Now, I can understand a person not wanting to get the ladder out twice, but it's almost like we're forgetting Thanksgiving completely. I don't see anything wrong with turning on Christmas lights the first of December or even the last few days of November. But it seems like we could at least give Thanksgiving its due. If it were up to me, I'd ban Christmas carols and commercials until the Friday after Thanksgiving, but it's not up to me and I'm sure all the merchants are thankful for that.

"That's all well and good," said the unidentified voice at the other end of the phone line. "But what's that got to do with your lights still burning on the fifth of January?"

Well, I struggled for an answer, we're kind of funny people at our house. The woman who tells me when to put them up, when to take them down, when to turn them on and when to turn them off likes to leave them up until the Twelfth Day of Christmas. Or maybe it's the 12th of January. Whatever.

We enjoy the bright lights, greenery, red bows and all the other stuff so much we just hate to take them down and stuff them back into boxes. People just don't seem to be as happy and friendly once the Christmas season is over.

Heck, we left our outside lights up until near the end of February one year. Of course, that was back in the early '70s when there was so much snow and ice that only an idiot would have been on a ladder taking lights down. And we didn't turn them on very often. Usually, it was when one of the kids hit the switch by mistake.

"Well, . . .," my caller tried to get a word in edgewise. But it was no use. I was on a roll now.

Besides, I lectured, January and February usually are pretty dull months. Anything that can be done to brighten them a little should be more welcome. And my Christmas lights aren't intruding on any other holiday as they would be if they were burning the fourth Thursday in November.

We won't have another legal holiday until Martin Luther

King Day on Jan. 15, I rambled on, and I sure won't have my lights on then; that might be considered disrespectful. But if my lights are still up on Groundhog Day, and they just may be, I might turn them on. If there are any groundhogs on our hill, they might get a kick out of them.

"After that . . .," I started to say . . .

Click. The phone line went dead.

January, 1996

Resolved: Check this in a year

It's time for a change.

Not politically. That's little more than an exercise in futility. When a politician says it's time for a change, what he (or she) really means is that it's time to get rid of whoever's in office now and give me a chance to screw things up even worse.

Then it's time for another change. In politics, it's always time for a change.

When you talk about change this time of year—when December is about ready to give way to January, the old year is preparing to head for the door and make room for the new—you're talking about (Ugghh! Gag! The mere thought makes you want to throw up!)—New Year's resolutions.

What a waste of time. It must get awfully dull between Dec. 25 and Jan. 1 to make a person even think about New Year's resolutions. But I am. Just call me Mr. Dull.

The last time I greeted a new year with resolve was 1950. On Dec. 30 of that year I met a young woman at a basketball game. Hey, I completely lost it. I resolved right then and there that she was going to become a permanent part of my life. And she did.

I've often wondered ever since if that's why I quit making resolutions. End of subject; no further comment.

Anyway, I've always ridiculed resolutions. Two years ago, I wrote:

"In a good year, some of those resolutions lasted well into the second week of January. By Groundhog Day, all had been broken, if not forgotten."

It's true, you know. Oh, some extremely strong-willed people can say they're going to quit smoking, lose weight, quit cussing, climb Mt. Everest or some other similarly impossible feat and then do it. Ninety-nine out of a hundred of us can't.

But I have to do something. Time's growing short. Simply put, I've got to get my act together.

For instance, the computer I'm writing this on has a modem on it. A modem is supposed to let my computer talk to other similarly equipped computers. But my computer isn't on speaking terms with anyone. Maybe it has bad breath. Or B-O. Or perhaps it speaks a foreign language.

That's not right. My computer will develop a complex if, after more than two years since modem installation, it doesn't make some friends, come out of its shell and lead a normal life. Resolved: In 1992, I'm going to get that sucker working.

No. 2: In the last three months, I've bought at least 12 books, maybe one or two more. I've read one of them. "Why do you buy books if you're not going to read them?" asks the woman who picks them up and dusts them. Good question. In the coming year, I have to start reading some of them. One a week, perhaps. Or every two weeks. A month . . . or maybe one a year.

No. 3: Clean out that blankety-blank garage. We've lived here 32 months and there's parts of it that remain virtually unexplored. How bad is it? Well, the neighbors pull their shades when they hear our garage door opening. Some action must be taken, and some will be taken. Just as soon as it gets warmer.

No. 4: Quit procrastinating. I learned early on in this business not to put off until 9 o'clock what can be written at 8. Because you never know what big story might break at 10 or 11. I practiced that faithfully for 40 years or more. But then came retirement. Now, it's more like never put off until tomorrow what you can put off until next week. Or next month. Next year?

My list could go on and on. Yours could too. Go ahead and make one. Maybe New Year's resolutions aren't so bad after all.

I made only four, so if I succeed on just one of them, I'm batting .250. Have you noticed lately the kind of multimillion big bucks contracts .250 hitters are signing these days? Go for it!

December, 1991

Happy birthday to all of U.S.!

The isolated POP! of a firecracker or two has punctured the sticky stillness of the last few hot summer nights.

Not really loud. Unless you're sitting on the porch, dozing a little before bedtime. These babies are only about an inch and half long and no bigger around than a drinking straw.

Never mind that the manufacturer calls them something like "Thunder BOMB" and has a bolt of lightning printed on the package right above where it warns "CAUTION-EXPLOSIVE. Do not hold in hand. Lay on ground, light fuse, get away. Use outdoors under adult supervision only."

That's just there because the government requires it. Did you ever see a kid stop and read what's on the label before tearing into a package of firecrackers? Of course not. This is July. School's out. Reading is for September through May.

The noise level increases manyfold on the Fourth of July.

That's THE day. The Fourth of July turns just about everyone into a kid again, even the cranky old guy next door. This is the day you let it all hang out.

Some folks can make an awfully strong case for the Fourth as their favorite holiday of the year. Sure, they concede, Christmas is the biggie, the one you wait a whole year for.

But Christmas lays some heavy stuff on you, too. Such as making you think about the true meaning of the day. It's better to give than receive and all that which makes you take off on a guilt trip every time you open a gift bigger, prettier or more expensive than the ones you bought.

But not the Fourth of July. You don't have to buy presents or mail cards. Think real hard, when was the last time you got a Fourth of July card?

The Fourth is party time, plain and simple. Just like a big birthday party, which is exactly what it is: Independence Day, our nation's birthday, its 215th. Recall what happened in the Persian Gulf last January and February and we've got plenty to celebrate.

It's party time, indeed!

You hear firecrackers from the time you wake up, even shortly before. It's one big picnic. Hot dogs, hamburgers, potato salad, ice cream, watermelon. Eat, drink and be merry, for tomorrow we may diet.

You don't even have to go to church on the Fourth of July, except every six or seven years when it falls on a Sunday.

If you've been around for, say a fourth of the country's birthdays, more than likely at least once you'll say, "It's been a nice day, but the Fourth isn't what it used to be."

And it isn't. But what is?

The Fourth has become victim of laws that say people can manufacture and sell fireworks but it's against the law to buy them and set them off unless you have a million dollars worth of insurance to pay for any possible damage.

Once upon a time, there were fireworks stands all over southern Ohio. And if you couldn't find them in Ohio, they always were plentiful in Kentucky.

All day long you'd hear POP! POP! POP! at isolated intervals from those who wanted to make their firecrackers last as long as possible. Then someone would light a whole package at once and give you POP!POP!POP!POP!POP!POP!POP!POP and neighborhood dogs would howl and cats would streak under the bed or up a tree.

Someone would get some of those big round red ones about the size of your thumb and there'd be a contest to see who could set one off under a can and make the can fly the highest into the sky.

When it got dark, the Roman candles and skyrockets and

186

other things kids couldn't afford lit up the skies.

The Fourth of July was a great day. Still is when you think a little about it.

July, 1991

Thankful this day comes only once a year

Sunday dinner? It looked a lot like tuna-noodle casserole. No one's really certain. It was something that was pushed to the rear of the refrigerator sometime in the past and nearly was forgotten.

Is that green stuff Jell-O? Could be. It also could be mold. Who knows? Isn't that how someone discovered penicillin once upon a time? We may be on the threshold of greatness here.

You see, what this is all about is that late November is the only regularly scheduled fridge-cleaning time that is observed by nearly everyone everywhere.

Most refrigerator cleanings are a matter of choice. The woman in charge of this task usually declares, "Well, I have several things I could do today. I could (1.) wallpaper the bedrooms, (2.) go in for that root canal or (3.) clean the refrigerator.

"I know what I'll do, clean the refrigerator!"

But at this time of the year, there is no choice. It's mandatory that she get a chisel, a shovel, several garbage bags and go to it.

Some of what's in there is still edible, or at least looks that way. That's why we have dishes known as Something-or-other Surprise. Serves two.

We have to make room for the turkey!

So exit the leftovers. Take out the pickles, mustard, ketchup, jellies, all that stuff that won't spoil. We'll find someplace to put the turkey and all that goes with it. Get those soft drinks out of there, they take up a lot of room.

"What are you trying to sneak back in there?" demands the warden. "This Bud's for the basement. We don't have room for that here."

Finally, there's room for a bird that looks big enough to feed Stormin' Norman and half of the Saudi Arabia vets, many of whom weren't home this time last year.

Do we really need a turkey that big? I know, let's buy a live one this year. I learned the tomahawk chop during the playoffs and the World Series. I bet Jane Fonda doesn't have a frozen turkey in her refrigerator.

You don't really need a turkey that big, you know.

There's something magical about turkeys that make them grow larger after they're cooked. They're like protozoa or amoeba or whatever you call those things that reproduce themselves. Sort of like rabbits.

It's a known fact that if you don't eat both turkey drumsticks on Thanksgiving Day, there will be four of them in the refrigerator the next day. If you aren't extremely careful, you will be up to your gizzard in drumsticks and other turkey parts by the Twelfth Day of Thanksgiving.

Ditto for the dressing. Or do you call it stuffing? Whatever. You can't get rid of it. Some of that green, fuzzy stuff we put in the garbage bag the other day may have been dressing/stuffing from last year.

Why do our wives insist on filling our plates with something that has been up a turkey's butt for six or eight hours?

Anyone for a pizza.

In the immortal words of Johnny Paycheck, you can take this bird and stuff it!

November, 1991

14—30-

The title of this chapter

is newspapers' time-honored

symbol for the end of a story.

The stories of five people who

played important roles in my

life ended in the last few years.

I was very fortunate to have known

them.

A teacher who taught me a lasting lesson

Teachers leave lasting impressions on the young people they meet in their classrooms. Good teachers leave long-lasting impressions.

Fern Curry Wheeler, who died last week just 30 days shy of her 93rd birthday, was a good teacher. One of the very best.

She left a long-lasting impression on me. In more ways than one.

Of course, Miss Wheeler left lasting impressions on hundreds and hundreds of young people who attended Glenwood High School in the former steel mill town of New Boston where I grew up. After all, she taught there 36 years—from 1923 when she was only 23 years old until retiring in 1959.

You figure out how many students passed through Glenwood's halls during that time. Just remember, that was when New Boston's population was twice what it is now.

And you can be sure that Miss Wheeler had at least some effect on every child in school while she was there, whether they were in one of her classes or not.

It wasn't easy to miss one of Miss Wheeler's classes. Although best remembered as a teacher of Latin, math and English, she also at one time or another was in front of business English, civics and history classes. She also was a class adviser in addition to many other extracurricular clubs and activities.

I used to think it was unique that Miss Wheeler was one of my mother's teachers in the four years ending in 1930 and one of mine in 1945-46. Then I realized she probably taught the parents of every one of her later-year students—unless they had just moved into town.

Glenwood had some truly outstanding teachers in the mid '40s. I won't name any because I would certainly leave out some of the best and that would be a grievous error. These people were tough, no-nonsense teachers. They expected respect and they got it.

That's a lesson I learned in one of Miss Wheeler's classes the hard way.

It was plane geometry, one of my two classes with her that year. The other was sophomore Latin. She made both of them interesting, but to this day I haven't a clue why I took either one. I haven't said—or written—a word in Latin during all of my nearly 50 years working in newspaper factories. Nor have I ever done anything that called for the use of plane geometry.

We sat around tables in the geometry class and my chair backed up to Miss Wheeler's desk. The class was particularly slow coming to order that day and I probably was one of the reasons. I was, I am ashamed to admit, a motor-mouthed smart aleck.

Miss Wheeler, standing directly behind me, made one final

appeal for quiet. I wised off. KA-POW! Her right hand rung my right cheek.

I wised off again.

KA-POW! Her left hand did the same to my left cheek.

I never said another word the rest of the hour. Neither did anyone else in the room. Except Miss Wheeler. We probably learned more geometry that day than any other that year.

"So you were the one," Miss Wheeler's daughter said to me when I visited the funeral home. "She never forgot that and felt so bad about it. She said it was the only time she ever lost her cool in the classroom."

But, Miss Wheeler, you really didn't lose your cool. You were only doing what you had to do, what any good teacher of that era would have done. I deserved it, and if my Dad had ever learned what happened that day, I really would have caught it when I got home. But he never found out.

If that happened today, of course, you probably would have lost your job and faced a law suit. And if Dad had walloped me when I got home, some do-gooder would have nailed him for child abuse.

What a pity!

I'm glad I went to school when I did and I'm glad I had teachers such as Miss Wheeler who would discipline me and my classmates when we needed it.

I'm sorry, Miss Wheeler, that you remembered that little incident and felt badly about it all those years. Any hard feelings I ever had were gone as quickly as the sting and redness left my cheeks.

Only fond memories of an excellent teacher remain.

March, 1993

Lewis is dead and I feel rotten

It wasn't as if I had lost my best friend. I really didn't know Lewis Grizzard. Nor was it because his death a week ago was not expected. Just about anyone who ever heard of the man and cared the least little bit about him knew he had been living on borrowed time for the last year. Probably longer.

The Good Lord gave Lewis a defective heart when he was born 47 years ago, and it was only because the Man Above was fond of the skinny, weak-eyed little rascal that he hadn't checked out perhaps a dozen years sooner.

Still, when the young woman on TV told me Lewis Grizzard had died in an Atlanta hospital—mispronouncing Grizz-ARD as GRIZZ-erd—she left me with a really funny feeling in my stomach.

To paraphrase the title of one of his books written after the death of Elvis Presley, "Lewis Is Dead and I Don't Feel So Good Myself."

I had met him only once or twice. Probably only once, because I can't remember the second time and even allowing for age, if there had been another time, I would have remembered it.

Lewis came to Troy, Alabama (where I was trying to teach college students how to become newspaper reporters) for a speaking engagement. He packed the auditorium, something that usually happened only at graduation time.

Before his talk, he was kind enough to come over to the journalism building and talk with the student chapter of the Society of Professional Journalists and the newspaper staff. I don't remember what he said, but I do know I was the oldest person there to get his autograph.

Reading the wire service report of Grizzard's death, I learned that he "delighted and sometimes enraged readers."

Enraged? That's a pretty harsh verb, I would think. Upset would be more appropriate. Or ticked off. Maybe teed off, or perturbed if you prefer something fancier.

But enraged? Anyone enraged by Lewis Grizzard's writings had to be extremely thin skinned. Actually, what he did most of the time was to hold a mirror up in front of us and some of us didn't like what we saw. So we blamed him.

That's what he did in his second from last book, "I Haven't Understood Anything Since 1962 and Other Nekkid Truths."

In the very first chapter, Grizzard took dead aim at what he called the Speech Police and by Page 11 had his sights set on political correctness.

"It means keep your mouth shut, even if it is true, because we don't care about truth anymore," he wrote. He cited a page or two of examples, then added: "Say anything like that and you are politically incorrect, which also means you are racist, sexist, homophobic, etc., and you probably are for giving drug traffickers the death penalty."

Grizzard concluded the chapter: "And you know what else? I think there are a lot of other people like me, sick of the Speech Police, sick of being afraid to speak the truth, sick of groups like the Queer Nation, the ACLU and the National Association of Women Who Would Just Like to Beat the Hell out of Every Man They See.

"Sick of whining, more than anything else. Whine, whine, whine, bitch, bitch, bitch. It's become the national pastime."

Maybe Grizzard did enrage a few people, after all.

But not all. His columns appeared in 450 newspapers, and said one reader: "I felt like I knew him though I never met him. He came from the heart and he really knew how to get to you."

Jim Minter, one of Grizzard's former editors and best friends, saluted him: " . . . (He) drew more readers to his newspaper columns than anyone I've ever known, and had more loyal fans than any newspaper writer I've ever known; and . . . I've gotten more laughs from Lewis than I have from Mark Twain, and about as much wisdom."

The woman who shares my newspaper expressed some surprise that the three-times-divorced Grizzard had married again only four days before his death and wondered aloud why.

Probably because he loved the woman, for one thing, and for another, he probably was still seeking a marriage that wouldn't be ended by divorce.

March, 1994

A newspaperman's newspaperman

John G. Green, 89, a former editor of the Portsmouth Daily Times, died . . .

Why was I stunned when I read that the other day? Why did I feel as if a very large fist had just struck a very hard blow into my stomach?

Certainly, Mr. Green's death should have been no surprise. After all, as the news story said, he was 89. And, as baseball legend Casey Stengel supposedly once remarked when questioned about continuing to manage after getting along in years, "most people my age are dead."

But Mr. Green was the kind of man you kind of sort of expected to live forever.

What a loss! Not only to his wife, son, grandchildren and great-grandchildren, but also to all of those who ever worked for him, competed against him or just knew him. His death was a tremendous personal loss to many and equally a professional loss to many, many more.

Mr. Green—I don't ever remember addressing him any other way—was a newspaperman's newspaperman. OK, so that's a cliche. But there's no other way to describe him. He was good.

Newspapering has changed since Mr. Green left my home town in Ohio in 1957. That was about two years after the Daily Times had moved into a brand new building just a few doors away from the county courthouse and only a block from what was then a bustling downtown business district. Before that, it had been squeezed in among an auto showroom on the north, the bridge across the Ohio River to Kentucky on the west, a row of modest homes on the south, overshadowed by the floodwall that was built years too late.

All of that, except the bridge, is gone now, leveled and cleared away to make room for a new state university that is the community's brightest hope for economic rebirth. John Green, who was a proud graduate of Ohio's largest university, would have been proud of the new school. He would have reported its growth in his news columns and supported it strongly on his editorial page.

In Mr. Green's day, newspaper plants were noisy and dirty. Reporters used typewriters and paper, now they use computers. Type was set in molten lead, which solidified and was placed in a page form. Now it's done by even more computers, printed out on slick paper and pasted onto a page form.

A lot of other things have changed as well, but it takes younger people to understand them . . . and explain them.

When Mr. Green was a young telegraph editor in Canton in the 1920s, state, national and international news came into the newspaper from the wire services on teletypewriters, which accounted for much of the noise in a newsroom.

The telegraph editor usually was the first at work every morning, greeted by yards and yards of news copy printed out on seemingly endless rolls of paper about 10 inches wide. His first task of the day was to scan the copy, evaluate it and cut it into separate stories with the help of a long pair of scissors.

Mr. Green worked quickly with those big, sharp scissors. Too quickly for a man wearing a tie that hung to his belt. The loss of a tie or two to those shears prompted him to begin wearing a trademark bow tie that earned him the nickname of Johnny "Bow-Tie" Green.

The passing of a man such as John G. Green will stir memories of so many war stories, far more than there is room for here today. He will be remembered fondly, along with three of his contemporaries—W. P. "Pete" Minego, best known as a sports writer but a man who could find a news story anywhere he went; Ernie Schusky, a city editor who his town better than anyone else, and L. W. "Bill" Burns. If John Green was a newspaperman's newspaperman, and he was, then pipe-smoking Bill Burns was a reporter's reporter.

Few, if any, small-town newspapers ever had four editors and reporters that could have matched their skills. Those of us who were younger—and we all were—didn't fully realize until many years later what a talented group of people we had the opportunity to work with. John Green was the first editor I ever worked for. (He wouldn't have allowed me to end that sentence with a preposition.) He also was the best editor I ever worked for.

I wonder what I would have become if I had not met John Green in the summer of 1946. I was getting ready to begin my junior year in high school and listened to some football-playing friends complain about what they thought was lack of newspaper coverage of their school.

I wrote to Mr. Green—in longhand, because I didn't know how to type and didn't have a typewriter anyway—and asked if I could write high school sports for the newspaper. He wrote back—because we didn't have a phone—and asked me to come in and talk with him.

That was 48 years ago this coming football season. Thanks, Mr. Green, for introducing me to my life's work. It was one of the two best things that ever happened to me.

June, 1994

The most learned man I ever knew

As soon as I recognized the voice on the other end of the phone—and that was almost instantly—I knew what I was going to hear.

But first there was the usual exchange of pleasantries. "How are you getting along?" "Fine, and how about you? Haven't seen you at any basketball games this year."

You know, the usual small talk. Anything to prolong the inevitable. It was nearing 10 o'clock on a Sunday evening, hardly the normal time for a "how are you?" call.

And then it came. I don't remember the exact words at all, and that's unusual. Nearly a half century of talking to people in the news-gathering process had trained me to remember quotes just as they were said. But not this time. I doubt that my caller can remember exactly what he had said either.

Woodi Ishmael had died at his home in Florida, the caller told me. We both were shaken. It was not totally unexpected. Still, it was as if the caller's fist had jabbed through that portable phone and slugged me right in the stomach. Just below the heart.

We—the caller and I—had gone through this same drill just a little less than two years ago. The message then was that Gwen, Woodi's wife of just under 56 years, had died just a few days before Easter. Deja vu.

The caller and a declining number of others in our town had known Woodi nearly all his life. They remember him when he was a kid growing up. Some of them attended Lincoln School with him, even more were his classmates at Portsmouth High School. Then, after he had attended art school in Cleveland and went on to become one of his generation's finest painters, they entertained him in their homes when he and Gwen came home for visits that were far too infrequent.

I was a definite Johnny-come-lately in the friends department. I had met Woodi—for a minute or two—once back in the late '50s, I think it was, on one of his hometown visits. He already was famous in his field; I was a kid reporter mainly interested in sports. When it came time to interview and write about Woodi Ishmael, the assignment went to an older and more polished writer.

195

But in the 1980s, Woodi and I (and our wives, of course) wound up in the same town, Troy, Ala., and teaching at the same school, Troy State University.

Our first meeting was in the check-out line at the Winn Dixie. Although nearing 70, Woodi had just a few weeks before played the part of Big Jule, I think it was, in a summer theater production of the musical "Guys and Dolls." We talked about that briefly and promised to get together.

Over the next six years, we talked about a lot of things—in our home, in the Ishmaels' home, in Woodi's studio and in the Student Center grill at Troy State.

It didn't take long to recognize that this man knew more about more things than any one I'd ever met. And why not? He had traveled on six continents and had met world leaders as well as the man and woman on the street. A listing of the famous people, places and things he had put on canvas and paper with his paint brush would sound like a who's who, a what's what or a where's where.

Woodi could sit for hours, very dry martini in hand, and hold you spellbound with tales of whatever subject he chose to discuss. He had been there, he had done it or seen it . . . and more than likely had painted it.

A mandatory retirement age of 70, since lifted, caught Woodi at the end of the 1984 spring quarter. And approximately six weeks later he was diagnosed with lung cancer. The lung was removed, but Woodi was never the same. He said he would never pick up a paint brush again, and as far as I know he never did. He should have. He still had so much talent, so many more pictures to paint . . . but the desire was gone.

We left Alabama in 1989 and returned to Ohio. The Ishmaels left there a year later and moved to Florida to be near their only daughter and her family.

Gwen had wanted to go sooner, but Woodi stubbornly refused. Finally, Woodi's feisty wife spelled it out in terms he could understand.

"Woods (as she sometimes called him), you can stay here if you want to, but I'm going to Florida," she declared.

"OK," Woodi answered, "let's go."

The flabbergasted Gwen asked why he had resisted so adamantly for so long, then caved in so easily.

"Well," Woodi explained, "you never had put it to me that way before."

The 22 months Woodi and Gwen were apart since her death is the longest they had been separated since their marriage in 1937. Now, they're back together again.

And that's the way it should be.

February, 1995

Erma knew how to humor us

The death of Erma Bombeck in San Francisco "from medical complications following a kidney transplant" took a lot of laughter, happiness and fun out of a world that needs all of those things it can get.

Erma's humor column didn't appear in every daily newspaper in the United States, only about 600 of them. It just seemed like her unique brand of humor—the kind you read and identified with—was in every newspaper that rolled off the presses, no matter where you lived.

I have a file folder marked "Columns." In the pocket marked "B" are more than a dozen of Erma's. Few of them are dated, but you can get an idea of how old they are from the various shades of fading and the different hairstyles in Erma's accompanying photos.

The oldest, by my figuring, was written not too many years after Erma began writing for the Journal Herald in Dayton, Ohio, in the mid-1960s. It was about the women who have put their husbands through school and say, "Maybe next year I'll go back to school."

She ticks off the accomplishments of famous women—from Shirley Temple Black to Grandma Moses—who achieved fame later in life. She finally decided, "It's my turn." Erma was 37 years old at the time.

That clipping was a constant reminder that helped me return to college in 1977 at the age of 46.

Erma's columns—and her half dozen or so books—were sources of inspiration and reminders of so many things we too often take for granted.

Two were tributes to the father she lost when she was only 9. I was considerably older when mine joined hers, but I found it easy to identify with those columns. That was part of the beauty in Erma's writings: She could put your feelings into her words.

There's another any parent can identify with. Under a headline, "Growing pains affect parents more than kids," Erma recalls her own three children struggling for survival.

"Every time they asked for help, we told them we couldn't possibly deny them the poverty they so richly deserved because it builds character. We didn't want them to miss a single day of the struggle in pursuit of the American dream.

"The rhetoric was easy. Sitting by and watching is the hard part. I hate it."

Other columns pass along some of Erma's advice as a commencement speaker and a recollection of one of her three's completion of college. Two tips she offered collegians were: "Pursue every roach as if it were female, pregnant and crazy to come home with you in your luggage."

"Use a few big words once in a while so your parents will think they're getting their money's worth."

Erma was at her writing peak during the women's movement and her self-deprecating columns sometimes rankled the real die-hard libbers. In truth, Erma probably did more for women with her humor and laughter than those who marched, protested and burned their bras.

Just as most of us in the newspaper-writing business did, Erma got her feet wet by writing obituaries.

But she quickly switched to writing a column when "I realized that I was incapable of staying with the facts."

And she made it seem so simple, so easy, so effortless.

If God would have allowed Erma to come back and write one more column about her own death, she would have been able to find some humor in it. That's the kind of writer and the kind of person Erma Bombeck was.

April, 1996

About the Author

Jim Joseph began his career as a writer as a 15-year-old high school junior. Two weeks before the beginning of the football season, he convinced the editor of his hometown newspaper that he was just the person to write up games for one of the four local schools. It wasn't as auspicious start. His first cliche-filled story credited one of the home team's two touchdowns to the wrong player.

Still, it was the beginning of a 50-year career as a newspaper reporter, editor and columnist in Ohio, Kentucky, Indiana and Alabama. He also was a journalism professor at Northern Kentucky University and Troy State (Ala.) University. And he hopes to continue writing in one form or another for at least a few more years.

A native Ohioan who left part of his heart in Kentucky and another part in Alabama when he returned to his home state a few years ago, Joseph is a graduate of Northern Kentucky University and received his master's degree in education from Xavier University in Cincinnati. A college dropout in the early 1950s he returned to school 25 years later after his three children had been graduated from the University of Kentucky.

He and his wife, Norma, to whom this book is dedicated, have been married 45 years.